Reducing
Risks
to Life

Reducing Risks to Life

Measurement of the Benefits

Martin J. Bailey

American Enterprise Institute for Public Policy Research
Washington, D.C.

Martin J. Bailey is professor of economics at the University of Maryland.

Acknowledgments

For their many helpful comments and suggestions on various drafts of this study I am indebted to Glenn Blomquist, Yale Brozen, Alan Dillingham, Glenn Hackbarth, James C. Miller III, John Morrall III, and Walter Oi. Errors and omissions that remain are my own.

Library of Congress Cataloging in Publication Data

Bailey, Martin J
    Reducing risks to life.

    (AEI studies ; 243)

      1. Industrial safety—United States—Cost effectiveness.
I. Title. II. Series: American Enterprise Institute for
Public Policy Research.
AEI studies ; 243.
HD7654.B34   658.38'2   79-15720
ISBN 0-8447-3346-6

AEI Studies 243

Printed in the United States of America

CONTENTS

1
Managing Resources to Maximize Lives Saved

During fiscal year 1979, the federal government proposes to spend more than $70 billion on health, safety, and pollution control programs—that is, on programs aimed at prolonging the lives of Americans.[1] The private sector spends an additional, unknown amount to meet health, safety, and pollution control goals; much of this spending is mandated by regulations.[2] Are these sums too little or too much, in the face of other urgent demands for the money? Would these sums accomplish more if they were allocated differently among the same general set of programs?

The answers that we give to these questions clearly depend on the *benefits* that result from the spending; the value of these benefits depends in turn on the value we attach to saving lives. Whether we do so directly or by implication, we place a value on human life. Effective resource management, aimed at getting the best possible results, depends on recognizing this evaluation and considering carefully what this value is. Until both public and government-induced private programs to save or prolong lives are appraised properly, we cannot know whether they represent money well spent. Preliminary evidence indicates that the *public and government-stimulated private resources now allocated to safety and health would save more lives if there were more effective government management and policy.*

---

[1] The figures include the following: Medicare and Medicaid, $41.1 billion; other health services, $4.4 billion; research, education, planning, construction, statistics, and so on, $6.9 billion; regulatory agencies affecting health and safety, $1.2 billion; health services for military personnel and veterans, $9.8 billion; pollution control, $7.4 billion. Office of Management and Budget, *Special Analyses, Budget of the United States Government, Fiscal Year 1979*, pp. 242-53, 289.

[2] Murray L. Weidenbaum, "On Estimating Regulatory Costs," *Regulation: AEI Journal on Government and Society*, May/June 1978, pp. 14-17, provides partial estimates of some of these costs for 1976.

Effective resource management depends on measuring the costs and the benefits of alternative programs and selecting that set of programs and levels of spending that gives the greatest excess of benefits over costs. Effective management of health and safety programs therefore depends on measuring the benefits from lives saved and improved health and safety. How seriously we undertake this task depends in part on whether we think that efficient resource management is a practical goal or one worth striving for. We all question the effectiveness and wisdom of many government programs, but we may despair of improving them or may believe that other issues are more important. We also object to flagrant waste, particularly of resources devoted to attaining our primary objectives. The discipline of measuring benefits and costs locates waste, helps determine priorities, and can result in increased benefits.

In the realm of life-saving programs, the meaning of "waste" may be unclear; it may seem that the objectives of such programs are so overriding that procedures like measuring benefits and costs are superfluous. Yet priorities are no less a matter of concern here than in other areas. Waste reduces effectiveness, and reduction or elimination of waste will increase the number of lives saved. Hence a genuine concern for our goals requires that we give careful consideration to the measurement of benefits and costs of life-saving programs.

Levels and Trends of Mortality

What potential benefits can government programs, regulation, and research provide us? For an informed estimate we must look at past and present data relating to health and safety.

Figure 1 shows striking declines in death rates for various age categories from 1930 to 1975. In medicine and public health, strides have been made in the prevention and treatment of childhood diseases, and death rates from accidents have declined, probably in part because of the greater availability of emergency medical care.[3] Although the death rate has fallen for all ages, the relative declines were systematically greater in the younger age groups, including those not shown in Figure 1, and were most sharp in the youngest categories. This tendency probably reflects both a greater sense of urgency about preventing the deaths of children and young adults and a technical fact that the causes of their deaths have been easier to control. The overall improvement, adjusted to the population age distribution of 1940, is measured by the central line in Figure 1.

---

[3] U.S. National Center for Health Statistics, *Vital Statistics of the United States, 1940*, p. 15; and *1950*, pp. 169-81.

FIGURE 1
Death Rates for Selected Age Groups and Age-Adjusted Total Death Rate, 1930–1975

Death rate per 100,000 population

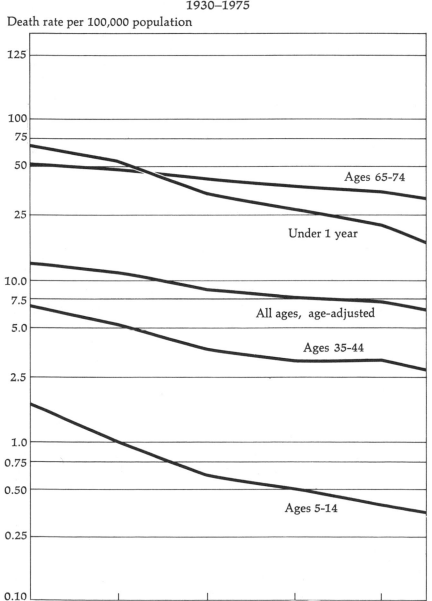

Source: *Vital Statistics of the U.S.* (various issues).

TABLE 1
U.S. Age-Adjusted Death Rates for Selected Causes
1960–1975

Cause	Death Rate (per 100,000 population)[a]		
	1960	1970	1975
All causes	760.9	714.3	638.3
Major cardiovascular diseases	393.5	340.1	291.4
Malignancies	125.8	129.9	130.9
Accidents	49.9	53.7	44.8
All other	191.7	190.6	171.2

[a] Weighted average rates using the population age distribution of 1940.
Source: *Vital Statistics of the U.S.* (various issues).

Table 1 shows U.S. age-adjusted death rates by major causes from 1960 to 1975. A marked, continuing drop in the age-adjusted death rate for major cardiovascular diseases contrasts with a slight rise in the death rate for malignancies. The age-adjusted death rate for accidents rose from 1960 to 1970, reflecting increases both in traffic deaths and in other accidental deaths. For several decades the number of deaths resulting from motor vehicle accidents per 100,000 population has increased. As incomes rise, people own more cars and drive more miles per 100,000 population, more than offsetting a steady improvement in highway safety measured in deaths per million of passenger miles. From 1970 to 1975, traffic deaths fell because of lower speed limits and curtailed travel after 1973. Other accidental deaths rose from 1960 to 1970 during the Vietnam War and then declined to 1975, repeating the pattern established in World War II of a wartime rise in accidental deaths for all age groups and a subsequent decline after the war.[4] The declining age-adjusted death rate for "all other" causes combines a sharp decline in the rate for infectious diseases with a partly offsetting rise from the remaining causes.

---

[4] This pattern reflects in part the cyclical nature of work injury rates. For a discussion of the reasons for this pattern see Robert S. Smith, *The Occupational Safety and Health Act: Its Goals and Its Achievements* (Washington, D.C.: American Enterprise Institute, 1976), p. 6.

Regulatory activities, research, and other government activities in the fields of health and safety aim to prolong life and to improve its quality by reducing the incidence of preventable illnesses and injuries. Some illnesses and injuries are considered beyond the reach of regulation and other governmental preventive activities, while others are particularly appropriate as targets for such programs. Job-related injuries have long been covered by state safety regulations and are now coming under federal regulation with the passage of the Occupational Safety and Health Act. More recent targets are cancer and other illnesses that may be caused by air and water pollutants. To provide further perspective, Figure 2 shows trends since 1910 in age-adjusted death rates for malignancies and for nonvehicular accidents, the latter for persons of working age (fifteen to sixty-four).

The slowly rising death rate for malignancies masks several cross-currents. The rise is partly spurious, especially before 1950, because of changes in definition and diagnosis. For example, the rise from 1940 to 1950 was partly because Hodgkin's disease and leukemia were first included in the category of "malignant neoplasms" in 1949. Furthermore, figures are "adjusted" by ten-year age groups, and increases in the average age within each group produce a small spurious increase in the death rate. Raw data, not age-adjusted, show a bigger rise over time because the fraction of the population in older age groups has increased, and old people have high cancer incidence.

Undoubtedly, there has been a genuine rise in deaths from lung cancer, associated with the growing percentage of smokers in the population, as well as other genuine increases. Furthermore, inasmuch as medical practice has advanced in the early detection, remission, and cure of most kinds of cancer, the slowly rising age-adjusted death rate indicates that there has been a rising incidence of cancer. For other kinds of illness, medical progress has sharply reduced death rates, and in the case of most serious infectious diseases preventive measures have reduced the number of cases as well. However, progress in treating cancer has not been great enough to lower the death rate in the face of increased incidence. As shown in Table 1, cancer is responsible for about one-fifth of all deaths. There are ample grounds for suspicion that major reasons for the increased incidence of cancer are chemicals, cigarette smoke, other pollution, and X-rays, to which the population has been exposed in increasing amounts. These sources of exposure are potentially controllable by regulation or other government intervention. Little is known at present, however, about the degree to which preventive measures, including regulation, could reduce the incidence of cancer.

FIGURE 2

AGE-ADJUSTED DEATH RATES FOR MALIGNANCIES
AND NONVEHICULAR ACCIDENTS, 1910–1975

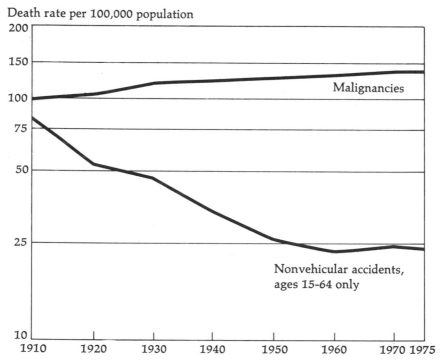

Death rate per 100,000 population

Source: *Vital Statistics of the U.S.* (various issues).

Accidental deaths present a different picture. Aside from the trend in motor vehicular accidents discussed earlier, deaths from other accidents have dropped sharply since 1910, although the rate has leveled off in the past fifteen years. In addition to improvements in medical care, factors that have reduced accidental deaths include improved job safety, at least into the early 1960s, and a reduction in the proportion of the population engaged in dangerous occupations, such as farming.

The trend in Figure 2 for nonvehicular accidents represents working-age persons only, but it is similar to that for the whole population. The death rates are higher for workers in paid employment or operating their own farms and businesses, although job-related accidents are only part of the total. For the whole population in these ages, job-related deaths are about one-third of total accidental deaths, or eight per 100,000 persons per year. About two-thirds of this age group are employed; thus among those employed the job-related accidental death rate is about twelve per 100,000 per year. Compared with the rates for malignancies and other causes of death, this rate is low. Many more accidents and accidental deaths occur off the job than at work. For all workers as a group, therefore, it is clear that the reduction of on-the-job accidents can no longer contribute substantially to their improved health and longevity. (Whether the same is true of a reduction in their exposure to harmful substances is not known at present because pertinent data are unavailable.)

For workers in unusually hazardous occupations, however, there is the possibility of significant improvement in overall death rates. Table 2 shows the risks of death from job-related accidents for workers in an average of hazardous occupations and for lumbermen, who face exceptionally high risks, and the resulting overall risk of death from all causes. Although these occupations may be unavoidably dangerous, it is conceivable that their safety could be significantly improved. Reduction in the risk of death from job-related accidents in relatively dangerous occupations would have more noticeable effects on overall death rates of workers in these occupations than for the average worker. For example, whereas a 10 percent reduction in all job-related deaths would reduce the death rate for all workers from all causes by a mere 0.2 percent, from 440 to 439, for lumbermen such a reduction would reduce their death rate from all causes by nearly 4 percent, from 696 to 669 per 100,000.

Fundamental Approaches to the Government Role

The approach this study applies to programs affecting health and safety is based on the belief that such programs should be purposeful, mutually consistent, and effective and that they should strike a well-considered balance with other citizen concerns, such as material well-being. In the interest of brevity I concentrate on ways to strike this balance in the existing set of programs and do not discuss the desirability of eliminating or adding programs. Also, the rationale for government intervention is outside the scope of this discussion.

Whenever programs are ill-considered and wasteful, one way to make all affected persons better off is to remove the waste and distribute the savings in cash to those affected, or to use the resources for programs that better serve them. The affected persons include those whose health and safety the programs improve, those who work in

TABLE 2
Death Rates in Ordinary and Hazardous Occupations
1975

	Death Rates per 100,000 Population		
	Average of all workers	Average of hazardous occupations	Lumbermen
All causes	440	550	696
Job-related accidents	12	122	268

Sources: Column 1: Calculated by author from *Vital Statistics of the U.S.* and from *Statistical Abstract of the U.S.* Columns 2 and 3: Job-related accidents from sample of thirty-three occupations reported in Richard Thaler and Sherwin Rosen, "The Value of Saving a Life," in *Conference on Income and Wealth, Household Production and Consumption* (New York: National Bureau of Economic Research, 1975); all causes calculated by adding the difference between the figures in Column 1.

government and in private business in support of the programs, and the taxpayers and consumers who pay for them. If all these persons can be made better off by better program design and management, they would presumably prefer this efficiency, provided they understood it. This study attempts to add to such understanding.

An alternative view is that in a diverse, democratic society consistent, well-considered decision making is both undesirable and impossible.[5] Certainly we can agree that the founding fathers consciously preferred wasteful representative government to efficient tyranny, as do we ourselves. However, this common view does not argue for more waste in government, and it gives no guidance whatever as to the degree of inconsistency, disjointedness, and consequent inefficiency necessary to prove a government's democratic credentials. Few would argue that whatever comes out of the political process is inherently good—that regardless of what policy our government adopts, this is the best of all possible worlds.

Moreover, this position that democratic government must be to some degree inefficient carries no weight either for or against the possible role in government of rational management with its weighing

[5] See, for example, Aaron Wildavsky, *The Politics of the Budgetary Process* (Boston: Little, Brown, 1974); his "The Political Economy of Efficiency," *The Public Interest*, no. 8 (Summer 1967), p. 30; and C. E. Lindblom, *The Intelligence of Democracy* (New York: Free Press, 1965).

of benefits against costs. Solid, well-organized information about costs and benefits and other management-oriented information sometimes affect political decisions. Although many river and harbor projects have held their own against conclusive proof that they were utterly wasteful, other programs have fallen by the wayside as a result of such solid information. The Department of Defense, especially, has a history littered with weapons programs and other projects canceled for good cause. Sometimes, although not always, effective weapons replace ineffective ones as a result of sound analysis. A recent example is the termination of the B-1 bomber in favor of the cruise missile. Information about costs and benefits can be used effectively or ignored, but it can be used only if it exists.

Programs affecting health and safety provide a major battleground for the controversy over efficiency in government management. The natural path for careless management, the path of least resistance, is to spend large amounts of public money and to force private firms and consumers to spend substantial amounts to avoid dramatic, highly publicized deaths such as those occurring in airline crashes and those resulting from the consumption of contaminated canned foods. Those causes of death that excite less attention, such as needless traffic deaths resulting from poorly designed highways and the like, are comparatively overlooked.[6] If one accepts the ongoing political process as poetry in motion, one acquiesces calmly in these inconsistencies. If, in contrast, avoidance of needless deaths through a set of effective government programs is one's goal, the view that knowledge is power must be brought into the public arena.

Although this point is straightforward, other related issues are more subtle. Persons exposed to particular risks may not know precisely what those risks are and may either overestimate or underestimate them. If wise government policy choices are closely related to the choices private citizens make, as they should be, should the government base its policy on actual risks or on perceived risks? Should the government reduce the actual frequency of tragedies, or should it simply make them less painfully obvious? Should the government concentrate on improving the perception and feeling of safety, rather than improving actual survival chances? The issue is further clouded because even with perfect knowledge of all risks, individual choices weigh risk against material benefit differently in

---

[6] This phenomenon has long been recognized. For a discussion see William G. Sumner, "The Forgotten Man," in A. G. Keller and M. K. David, eds., *Essays of William Graham Sumner* (New Haven: Yale University Press, 1934), vol. 1, p. 466.

different circumstances. Although there is no rational case for spending a huge sum to avoid a death from one cause while refusing to spend a relatively small sum to avoid a death from another cause, it can be shown that rational, well-informed citizens do not equalize these incremental sums precisely in private choices. Hence a policy based on such choices will allow some, albeit minor, differences in these sums to remain.

Whether the government should concentrate on actual rather than preconceived risks is itself an important question. Assuredly, representative government will, in part, reflect the myths and widely shared errors of judgment of its constituents, and expert opinion should not override the popular will. On the contrary, the myths and errors of judgment of experts in all parts of government, including those concerned with health and safety, are at least as troublesome as those of the representative citizen. One suspects that the U.S. electorate has acquiesced too freely already in delegating to experts powers of decision and control over private choices. The thrust of this study is that important myths and errors of judgment in public decisions affecting health and safety deserve to be corrected through better information and analysis. For instance, if publicity leads most people to exaggerate the risk of flying by commercial airline relative to the risk of traveling by auto, safety-oriented publicity could correct this apparently widespread error.

A tempting alternative approach, widely accepted by experts, interested groups, and political leaders, is to pursue a set of appealing fixed health and safety objectives "regardless of the cost." For example, in a discussion of the application of economic criteria to alternative health and safety regulations, a representative of the oil and chemical workers' union reportedly said, "Congress mandated very specifically that the workplace should be free of hazards. It didn't say the workplace should be free from hazards only if the employer could afford it, or only if it wouldn't cost him too much money."[7] In the process of enactment of some thirty or more regulatory acts during 1970–1975, and in the language chosen, there is little sign of congressional concern about the costs of compliance.[8] It is therefore to be expected that members of the public will find themselves paying considerably more for increased safety through regulation-mandated cost increases than

[7] Anthony Mazzocchi, quoted in the *Washington Post*, Thursday, May 12, 1977, p. A5.

[8] For a list of enactments and an analysis of the lack of concern about cost, see William Lilley III and James C. Miller III, "The New 'Social Regulation,'" *The Public Interest*, no. 47 (Spring 1977), p. 49.

they are willing to pay implicitly through the choice of a safer job, the choice of a safer mode of transportation, and so on.

An extreme example is the objective of "zero discharge" of pollutants into U.S. streams and lakes by 1985, mandated by the Federal Water Pollution Control Amendments of 1972. A recent estimate of the cost of meeting interim standards for 1983 under this law is $468 billion, plus whatever might be required to limit agricultural runoff.[9] A complete end to water pollution may be technically impossible; the capital cost of closely approaching this stated goal would quickly exceed one year's national product, and the operating cost would consume a substantial fraction of every year's product.

In fact, there is little chance that federal, state, or local governments will appropriate the funds necessary to rebuild and enlarge all municipal waste and sewage treatment facilities to the point that their only effluent into the streams is pure drinking water. Objectives of this kind threaten to impoverish the nation and will cause the electorate to call a halt. These resources may be utilized in other programs to save more lives and yield other preferred benefits, rather than to meet the 1983 interim standards for water quality.

An excellent, carefully researched example of the potential benefits of good management in the field of water quality control appears in the economic analysis of several water basins by Kneese and Bower.[10] For the Delaware Estuary they show both costs and benefits of alternative programs of water quality control up to a program of highly pure water (but short of "zero discharge") and of alternative means of achieving the objectives. Table 3 summarizes their overall results. For a program that achieves almost pure water everywhere in the estuary the discounted value of the long-term cost is $460 million; the discounted value of the benefits, which has a range of uncertainty, would be $160–350 million. Less ambitious programs cost much less,

[9] Allan V. Kneese and Charles L. Schultze, *Pollution, Prices, and Public Policy* (Washington, D.C.: Brookings Institution, 1975), p. 70. In its *Cost Estimates for Construction of Publicly-owned Wastewater Treatment Facilities, 1976 Needs Survey* (February 10, 1977), the Environmental Protection Agency cut this estimate to $150 billion by scaling down the interim control objectives sharply and ignoring the "zero discharge" goal.

[10] The principal benefit of improved water quality is more opportunities for swimming, fishing, and boating. These benefits can be obtained by better management, at a fraction of the cost of an indiscriminate, wholesale program. The economical way to protect health is through treatment of drinking water by the user community, not by making all streams and rivers pure enough to drink. See Allan V. Kneese and Blaire T. Bower, *Managing Water Quality: Economics, Technology, Institutions* (Baltimore: Johns Hopkins University Press, 1968), pp. 158–64 and 224–35.

TABLE 3
Costs and Benefits of Alternative Programs
for the Delaware Estuary

Purity Level	Discounted Present Values of Twenty Years (millions of 1968 dollars)		
	Costs under arbitrary regulation	Least-cost system attainable	Benefits
1	460	460	160-350
2	315	215	140-320
3	155	85	130-310
4	130	65	120-280

Source: Allan V. Kneese and Blaire T. Bower, *Managing Water Quality: Economics, Technology, Institutions* (Baltimore: Johns Hopkins University Press, 1968).

yet they would yield benefits almost as high as those of the most expensive program. For purity levels 3 and 4 the benefits would almost surely exceed the costs, especially for the lowest-cost approach; it is a toss-up whether level 3 or 4 should be chosen on efficiency grounds. Dropping the objective from level 1 to 3 would save two-thirds of the cost, reducing it from $460 million to $155 million under arbitrary regulation of the customary type. Shifting to effluent charges (described and analyzed by Kneese and Bower) or some other means of obtaining the least-cost fulfillment of the program would save almost half the remaining cost of level 3, reducing it from $155 million to $85 million; for level 4, these means would cut the cost of $130 million exactly in half. Under arbitrary regulation the costs of every program are greater than the possible benefits at the lower end of the range. Hence, taking care to find the right balance between benefits and costs and choosing the approach which attains the lowest possible cost for the benefits achieved is necessary to be sure of having a program in which benefits exceed costs.

A penetrating statement by the Council on Wage and Price Stability illustrates the same point in a rough way for the regulation of occupational health and safety. Commenting on a proposed standard for exposure to coke oven emissions, the council said:

Our analysis concludes that, at a minimum, this standard would cost $4.5 million per life saved. Whether to accept such costs is a matter for OSHA's judgment. We note, however, that this figure is extremely high, considering the amounts spent in other health and safety areas. If we were to spend $4.5 million per cancer death in an attempt to save all lives lost to cancer, we would commit ourselves to an annual expenditure roughly equal to our entire gross national product. Since we obviously cannot spend that sum, it is very important first to be sure that our cost and benefit figures are correct and second to be sure we understand why society is being asked to spend $4.5 million per life saved in this area of cancer prevention to the exclusion of other areas of cancer hazard. Putting it bluntly, at least we ought to determine whether this $241 million . . . or the more conservative estimate of $160 million per year in expenditure of real resources could not save more lives if it were expended on alternative programs.[11]

The Mounting Demands of Unrestrained Regulation

The estimates discussed above imply not only a misuse of resources in relation to the most effective ways to save lives but also an enormous potential drain on U.S. growth and on our material standards of living. As noted above, the estimated initial cost of meeting interim standards for pollutants in U.S. streams and lakes would be $468 billion for cities, towns, and industry, plus an uncounted and perhaps uncountable amount to control agricultural runoff. Achieving the goal of absolute purity would cost an additional huge but undetermined sum. The costs of achieving the best attainable standards of health and safety in the workplace and of limiting air pollution are also uncounted and difficult to determine. The annual operating cost for meeting these standards is estimated to be roughly one-third of the initial capital cost.[12]

The Occupational Safety and Health Administration has officially taken note of between 1,500 and 2,000 chemical and other substances as "suspect carcinogens"; for the handful of these on which OSHA has proposed regulations, the expected average annual cost of compliance is $267 million each. If costs this high were extrapolated to

11 Statement on behalf of the Council on Wage and Price Stability by James C. Miller III before the Occupational Safety and Health Administration (OSHA), Washington, D.C., May 11, 1976.

12 Based on Edward F. Denison, "Effects of Selected Changes in the Institutional and Human Environment upon Output per Unit of Input," *Survey of Current Business*, vol. 58 (January 1978), Tables 1 and 2, p. 26.

cover 1,500 carcinogens, the United States would eventually spend $400 billion per year, in addition to all other spending to control worker exposure to carcinogens.[13] If, on the average, control of one of these agents also controls a second (two for the price of one), U.S. spending to control this hazard would still come to $200 billion per year. If hundreds or thousands more suspected carcinogens are subsequently identified, the control costs will climb higher.

The partial, quite incomplete estimates discussed thus far imply annual costs of some $150 billion for the 1983 interim standards for control of water pollution (approximately one-third of $468 billion), plus some $200 to $400 billion for carcinogen control. Beyond these are costs associated with reducing other workplace hazards, controlling air pollution, meeting the goal of completely pure water, improving the safety of consumer products, and so on. Moreover, the costs would rise with continued growth in the U.S. economy. In a $2 trillion economy the listed costs of $350–550 billion would absorb from 17.5 to 27.5 percent of gross national product. If these costs were to be absorbed by lower real incomes of households (that is, with no cutback in government), standards of living would be reduced from 25 to 40 percent, based on the ratios of these costs to private disposable incomes. In addition, there are other uncounted costs. These numbers are highly extrapolative and will be revised with the development of more data. However, the magnitude indicated poses a real threat— one that it would be reckless to disregard. It seems unlikely that, in the face of mounting costs, the electorate will consent to this heavy an investment in health and safety.

The costs had begun to mount significantly by 1975. Costs of pollution abatement by business had at least doubled every two years after 1968. By 1975 these costs were running almost $10 billion on a current-cost basis outside of mining; the associated capital investment totaled between $2.5 and $3 billion annually. Together these operating costs and investment, plus smaller amounts for worker health and safety, reduced the growth rate of resource productivity in the United States by 0.36 percent in 1975, thus absorbing about one-sixth of the average growth rate of 2.1 percent per year.[14] These costs, though not yet dramatic, have risen enough in a short time to pose a clear threat for the future.

---

[13] See Statement of James C. Miller III, on behalf of Vistron Corporation, before OSHA, "Occupational Exposure to Acrylonitrile, Proposed Standard," Docket OSH-108, April 4, 1978.

[14] Denison, "Effects of Selected Changes," pp. 26, 36, and 41. See also Murray L. Weidenbaum and Robert DeFina, *The Cost of Federal Regulation of Economic Activity*, Reprint 88 (Washington, D.C.: American Enterprise Institute, May 1978).

2
The Logic of Benefit-Cost Analysis

The principle of economic efficiency for government projects is elegantly stated in the Flood Control Act of 1936. It requires that only those projects shall be submitted for congressional action for which the "benefits to whomsoever they accrue exceed their costs." This principle means simply that if those who benefit from a project had to bear its entire cost, they would consider it worth paying for. In a few cases, those who benefit do pay; fees at national parks pay for operations and improvements in the parks, and purchased electricity covers part of the costs of the TVA. In all other cases, if the benefits in fact exceed the costs, some enjoy the benefits of a worthwhile project at the expense of taxpayers nationwide. Where costs exceed benefits, those who benefit would reject the project if they were required to pay for it in its entirety. If the beneficiaries do not bear a significant share of the costs, however, they may favor such a project. The benefit-cost criterion requires that if benefits are less than the costs the project be dropped.

This logic applies to entire projects as well as to their various parts, features, and possible small modifications. Each aspect of a project should be chosen in such a way that the last dollar spent yields at least a dollar of benefits. For brevity I will henceforward take this point to be understood, and not repeat it in later references to the use of benefit-cost analysis.

The Need for Benefit Measurement

Despite the simple, obvious appeal of making the comparison of benefits with costs the decisive criterion for the adoption or rejection of projects, this method is often criticized. As a practical matter, our political system leads to the adoption of many government programs whose benefits are a small fraction of their costs, when the beneficiaries are politically powerful. Although those who benefit would reject the programs if they were obliged to pay all the costs, almost all programs are financed not by user charges but by the general fund, so that taxpayers nationwide bear the costs.[1] In many cases user charges are impractical. In several other cases where they are feasible, such as waterways, it has so far proved politically impossible to impose user charges that cover costs. Hence, many projects benefit a relatively narrow group of people and impose costs on all taxpayers. However, other programs affecting health and safety, such as basic medical research and nationwide control of air pollution, benefit nearly all taxpayers.

If a group of beneficiaries of a program or project is relatively small, and if it is either generally acceptable or politically necessary to confer benefits upon them, an alternative method of providing these benefits is through a straightforward cash payment. If the benefits of a program or project under consideration are equal to a small fraction of the costs, say, $10 million of benefits for $100 million of costs, all concerned would be better off if the government simply distributed $50 million to the same beneficiaries in the form of "special revenue sharing" or the like. This alternative would increase local benefits from $10 million to $50 million, while reducing the burden on the general taxpayer from $100 million to $50 million. Although this alternative, if used as a general rule, would increase the incentive to propose wasteful projects, its adoption would merely lead to an increase in transfer payments without wasting resources on the scale that occurs when we finance large numbers of projects with costs exceeding the benefits conferred. Moreover, the straight cash transfer would be reviewed by the appropriate criterion, namely whether the recipients are especially deserving; programs with other objectives, such as those improving health and safety, could be evaluated strictly on their merits. The scarcity of resources requires that such programs should be adopted only if they have benefits greater than their costs.

Although the political system seems to reject this logic and to choose projects in a nonrational way, an examination of the political limitations on making choices among alternatives is beyond the scope of this discussion. Whether the substitution of a straight cash transfer (or a better program) for a wasteful program or outright abandonment of the latter is politically feasible is a decision for the policy makers.

[1] See Allan Meltzer, *Why Government Grows* (Los Angeles: International Institute for Economic Research, 1976).

However, an accurate, unbiased assessment of benefits and costs, a detailed accounting of who benefits and who is harmed, and a careful setting-out of possible alternative programs with the corresponding information for each alternative can only help those faced with this task.

The benefits of a program are measured by the amount the beneficiaries would be willing to pay to obtain the goods and services provided by the program. In almost all applications of benefit-cost analysis this measure is the value of the goods and services in private markets. If a land reclamation project will increase wheat production, for example, its benefits are the revenue the added wheat will bring when sold less direct costs of production. The worth of some goods and services, such as health and safety, is harder to estimate because there is no direct way to purchase them in private markets. However, the principle is the same in this case as in the others: willingness to pay is the most reliable monetary measure of a benefit to a private household. Some information about this willingness is available, so that the approximate benefits of health and safety programs can be estimated in a straightforward way, just as in evaluating any other program.

Even if it were known precisely how much individuals are willing to pay to increase their own safety, many experts would reject this information for use in management of programs affecting health and safety. They would prefer using their own criteria for program selection and design with little regard to the measurement of costs and benefits. At issue is a basic question of the function of government: should the government provide the services people want, with due regard to cost? Or should the government provide the services that experts believe people need, whether they want them or not, and regardless of cost? Although the notion of what people want for themselves is less than perfectly clear in our political system, it can be defined with reasonable precision in terms of their observable choices of jobs and lifestyles. Such choices provide a basis for inferences about the voluntary choices they would make, if given the opportunity, regarding activities undertaken by the government. Managing government programs on this basis is measurably, perhaps enormously, superior to relying on experts' own views of what is best, which can be dangerous as well as wasteful. Program management based on an evaluation of costs and benefits that effectively reveal private valuations of program effects will achieve optimum results with the available resources.

Improvements in health and longevity in the past several decades have resulted both from private medical research and other activities and from public health service activities and government-sponsored research. In recent years the role of government has increased sharply, especially through the sweeping regulatory powers vested in OSHA and in the Environmental Protection Agency (EPA). Although regulations relating to health and safety have a long history, the sweep and scope of the new powers are unprecedented. Those who regulate can impose virtually unlimited costs on the private sector of the economy—they can reduce private standards of living without going through the legislative processes of enacting new taxes and appropriations.[2] The dollar estimates in the preceding section show the enormous potential threat of unbridled regulation. To limit wasteful and irresponsible demands by the new regulators, there is an urgent need for standards and procedures by which they would be required to weigh costs against benefits.

As a natural extension of the ongoing development of concepts and methods for estimating costs and benefits, analysts of particular programs have from time to time addressed the question of how to measure the benefits of saving or prolonging lives. However, there is an important distinction between values before the fact—those that apply in the planning and decision stage—and values after the fact. Suppose that in a population of 1 million persons the annual death toll of, say, 6,000 could be reduced to 5,000 by a health and safety program. It might appear that calculating a benefit per life saved means assigning a value to the life of each person whose life is prolonged by the program. At the time of evaluation, however, the identities of the persons who will be among the 6,000 who die without the program, and of those who will be among the 5,000 who die despite it, are unknown. Furthermore, the annual benefit of having the program is shared among all the population at risk at the beginning of each year, because they all face a reduced mortality risk. This reduction has a value to them which can be estimated. In contrast, there is no way to estimate a benefit for the particular persons whose lives are prolonged by the program, both because there is no way to know who they are and because there is no practical way for them to reveal how highly they value their lives—their maximum ransom.[3]

---

[2] See Murray L. Weidenbaum, "The New Wave of Government Regulation of Business," *Business and Society Review* (Fall 1975).

[3] For a clear discussion of this concept and its relationship to the value of safety concept used here, see Philip J. Cook and Daniel A. Graham, "The Demand for Insurance and Protection: The Case of Irreplaceable Commodities," *Quarterly Journal of Economics*, vol. 91 (February 1977), pp. 143-48.

Therefore, the pertinent "value per life saved" is simply a short-hand way to represent the total amount of benefits enjoyed by all the population whose risk is reduced, scaled for convenience in units of lives saved. In a group of 1,000 persons among the million just mentioned, the number expected to die each year will fall from six to five persons because of the proposed program; the sum of the amounts they are willing to pay for the lower risk can be viewed as the amount they collectively will pay to save one life. This amount can be estimated from purely private choices involving small risk reductions. Although the planning concept of interest is the widely shared risk reduction produced by a proposed program, to simplify calculations it is convenient to use the sum of individual benefits over a population with one less expected death as a "value per life," and then to multiply times the number of expected lives saved.

Moreover, the pertinent value of benefit per life saved can vary from case to case. For programs affecting the health and safety of the entire population a single average value serves well. Occasionally a different value may be appropriate. In principle, the amount per life saved that a given group of persons will pay to reduce risk is greater if the risk is higher; for example, when a whole town is threatened by radioactive wastes, its population shares a sense of urgency that would imply spending more than an average figure (per life saved) to reduce the hazard. Also, as incomes increase with economic growth, citizens are willing to spend more for health and safety. Similarly, comparison of a high-income group with a low-income group at a given date would reveal that the benefit of added safety, measured by willingness to pay, is higher for the high-income group. Occasionally a program evaluation will need to take such differences into account. As a rule, these differences will do no more than double or halve the average value.

Other Approaches and Criticisms of Benefit-Cost Analysis

An approach that provides a seemingly sophisticated alternative to benefit-cost analysis for improved safety suggests that decision makers should "minimax regret"; that is, they should minimize the chance of the worst thing that can happen.[4] Proponents of this view do not explain who decides what is the worst thing that can happen or the criteria for decision, but this approach provides a rationale for the official who carefully protects himself against a highly publicized failure and who pays scant attention to a steady stream of unpubli-

---

[4] Henry Owen and Charles L. Schultze, *Setting National Priorities* (Washington, D.C.: Brookings Institution, 1976), p. 469.

cized avoidable losses. For example, a drug official who plays it safe in this sense may block approval of ten drugs, one of which might harm 500 persons and cause a scandal, while the other nine drugs, if approved, would save 10,000 from death and disease, if the identity of the harmful drug and of those harmed by the unavailability of the other drugs cannot be predicted. Such behavior would scarcely be acceptable to a fully informed public. The criterion to "minimax regret" would seem to make a virtue of the anomalies that flow from poor information and from a political system that fails to hold decision makers responsible for the full consequences of their actions.

An alternative interpretation of the "minimax regret" or "play it safe" approach is less easily dismissed. When regulators decide whether to ban the emission of certain chemicals that may prove to be carcinogenic, they are choosing between immediate, comparatively certain costs of emission control and long-run, comparatively unpredictable costs of increased cancer. There are many regulatory issues of this general character. Some of these chemicals are no doubt especially dangerous, and others harmless; it will be a long time, at best, before their cancer-causing properties are known. The "minimax regret" rule says, in effect, to assume the worst for each chemical—to use the most damaging estimate possible of its potential harm. This rule has one undeniable merit: if analysis of a particular case shows that the costs of control are greater than any possible damage, the chemical would be allowed to be emitted, whereas traditional regulation would ignore the comparison of costs and potential damage and would force emission control if any significant harm were expected. However, the rule is irresponsible if applied generally. Carried to an extreme, it would create panic whenever anyone declares that the sky is falling. If the worst that can happen in fact comes to pass only one time in a thousand chances, and nothing serious happens the other 999 times, there must be a low limit to how much citizens would pay to protect against the worst in each and every one of the thousand chances. In contrast, if this worst outcome in fact comes to pass as often as 500 or 800 times in a thousand chances, it would make sense to buy full protection every time. Hence, it is not enough to know the worst that can happen; one must also try to judge how likely that worst outcome is. When that likelihood is taken into account explicitly, the "minimax regret" criterion is no longer used, and expected costs are balanced against expected benefits, with a hedge against uncertainty.

These points are closely related to the sharp criticisms of benefit-cost analysis that appear in the report of a Congressional subcommittee chaired by Representative John E. Moss.[5] This report complained that in decision making affecting health, safety, and the environment, the long-term benefits of regulation are highly uncertain, that even the immediate costs of compliance cannot be estimated reliably, and that all such estimates can be biased according to the interests of the person making the estimate. The report suggests that the use of benefit-cost analysis creates "a bias against the public interest," that is, against issuing new regulations. The report concludes that

> whenever benefit-cost analysis is used, all relevant factors must be considered in order to inform the decision maker's choice as fully as possible. If significant delay may result from this process, a different decision making technique should be used. Finally, whenever benefit-cost analysis operates to bias a decision (such as its application by the Environmental Protection Agency in making decisions to limit or prohibit hazardous use of pesticides), its use is inappropriate.

The first of these three sentences seems to suggest that if benefit-cost analysis is not used, the decision maker need not consider all relevant factors; surely that was unintentional. The second sentence implies that it is more urgent to issue regulations and restrictions quickly than to consider the consequences carefully and to translate them into benefits and costs; it is a demand that the regulatory process go full speed ahead, without information if necessary, and without regard to the public interest. The last sentence takes it as established beyond doubt that the inherent bias in analysis is against issuing regulations.

Compared with an utopian ideal of perfect knowledge, attempts at estimating benefits and costs of a policy do indeed suffer from all the problems that the Moss report alleges, and more. The report overlooks the problem that in a government regulatory agency the bias is usually in the direction of action rather than inaction, and toward overstatement of risks to the public rather than understatement. In any event, the use of benefit-cost analysis to aid regulatory decisions should be compared not with an ideal but with the practical alternative. Reckless issuance of regulations in disregard of the costs will damage the public interest if the benefits to health and safety are too small to justify the costs. While paying lip-service to the uncertainty about the long-run effects of suspected carcinogens and other pollutants, the

---

[5] U.S. Congress, House, Subcommittee on Oversight and Investigations of the Committee on Interstate and Foreign Commerce, *Federal Regulation and Regulatory Reform*, 94th Congress, 2d Session, October 1976, chapter 15.

21

report drives to conclusions that are valid only if the worst possible outcome will be the typical one. Carefully gathered, relevant evidence will indicate the likelihood of the worst outcome and will carry precisely the weight it should in a competent, disinterested analysis of benefits and costs.

Participation in the political process of persons affected by a program or regulation explains some of the biases correctly identified by the Moss report. The decision-making process is subject to these biases whether or not benefit-cost analysis is formally employed, and the best practical remedy is to keep this process as open as possible. The procedures of benefit-cost analysis force its authors to state their factual assumptions clearly and expose their possible biases to criticism and correction. Hence the official assessment of benefits and costs performed by the agency involved should be publicized before a final decision on a regulation or other policy, and it should then be revised when necessary in response to outside comment. If that means delay, so be it; prudent decision making takes time.

The alternative may lead to an outcome the authors of the Moss committee report would themselves scarcely prefer. Ill-considered rules and requirements issued under the philosophy that cost is no object will cause expenditures on health and safety to mount unacceptably until a political reaction forces a halt. In the resulting political standoff, some programs and requirements will be in place that cost enormous sums per life saved, while other programs that could save lives cheaply will be blocked. At this point, a large part of the resources actually devoted to health and safety will be wasted, and lives that could be saved with these resources will be lost. An informed public would prefer prudent, deliberative management.

A somewhat different point of view appears in a frequently cited article by Zeckhauser.[6] Zeckhauser rejects benefit-cost analysis (which he calls "Potential Pareto Improvements") as the sole criterion for policy decisions; he nevertheless says that "analysts can provide some basic building blocks so that the ultimate decision makers . . . can have some inputs for what they are doing." One of his reservations is that a program in which benefits exceed the costs may have unacceptable distributional consequences—that the wrong people may benefit—and that those who benefit may not be charged for the full cost of the program. However, he does not argue that the analysis

---

[6] Richard Zeckhauser, "Procedures for Valuing Lives," *Public Policy*, vol. 23 (Fall 1975), p. 427. See also Steven Rhoads, "How Much Should We Spend to Save a Life?" and Max Singer, "How to Reduce Risks Rationally," *Public Interest*, no. 51 (Spring 1978), pp. 75 and 95, respectively.

should therefore be suppressed or falsified. He contends that the public's concern about the acceptability of the process by which decisions are made may override a concern about waste; hence some programs may cost more than others per life saved, and an inefficient overall program may be adopted. But then Zeckhauser suggests that if the decision process is regularly wasteful, the public may reject it in favor of a process that results in efficient outcomes "with a degree of regularity." He concludes that "estimates of the values of lives inferred from market transactions may not be appropriate guides for government decision-makers," without specifying or supporting an alternative procedure. Instead, he says that "procedures for valuing lives must be developed that appropriately reflect not only considerations of process, but also such matters as anxiety, income distribution, and possibilities for compensation."

Zeckhauser offers no such procedure, and it is not clear why it would be either possible or desirable. The policy maker is concerned with process, income distribution, and so on, and knows that many factors must influence his decision. He is perfectly capable of thinking about them separately and, indeed, will perform better by considering these factors one at a time. It is helpful neither to him nor to good analysis to try to put all these eggs into a twisted basket falsely labeled "valuation of life." The straightforward procedure that meets all the requirements to which Zeckhauser refers (for he takes it for granted, as I do, that the analysis of costs and benefits is compatible with due process) is to value the benefit of reduced risk in the same way as wheat or labor—according to what people are willing to pay for them in private choices; to list the distributional impact of a program separately; to analyze different possible ways to finance the program, including user charges; and to let policy makers decide what weight to give to the various considerations. Correct and separate appraisal of costs and benefits permit policy makers and the public to know the net sacrifice of material welfare that will follow if distributional and other considerations dictate an inefficient choice.

The "minimax regret" view, the Moss report, and Zeckhauser's view, together with my comments on them, reflect in the specific context of benefit-cost analysis the broad philosophical disagreements discussed in the section on fundamental approaches to the government's role. In addition, there are alternative views that accept benefit-cost analysis without question but that differ from my views on valuation, procedure, and scope.

An alternative view closely related to the benefit-cost approach emphasizes efficiency and effectiveness in the use of whatever funds are available. Suppose that the share of each year's total government budget that can be devoted to improving health and safety and the compliance burden that can be imposed on the private sector over and above taxation are given and fixed amounts. There is at least some plausibility to a claim that these amounts are set by a political balance between the pressures to spend more and the pressures to spend less, affected only by major new events or striking new information. (To the extent that this view is true, it partially supports the Wildavsky viewpoint cited at the beginning of this study.) Then good management requires that these amounts devoted to improved health and safety be used as effectively as possible and that a "value of life" concept be used directly to aid in resource management.

To illustrate this point, suppose that the government wishes to save as many lives as possible and allocates $20 billion to programs and components affecting health and safety (not including Medicare and Medicaid). This sum covers those parts of flood control projects that contribute to saving lives, those costs of military aircraft that increase pilot survival, medical research, safety features of highway design, and so on. Suppose that half this total sum, or $10 billion, goes into activities that save 10,000 lives at a cost of $1 million per life saved—and that the other $10 billion goes into activities that save 500,000 lives—at a cost of $20,000 per life saved. Suppose further that if the second set of activities were expanded they would encounter a steadily rising cost per life saved; at a total spending level of $20 billion, 200,000 additional lives would be saved at a maximum cost of $80,000 per life. In that case, terminating the first set of activities, which save only 10,000 lives, and diverting the $10 billion previously spent on these activities into the second set would result in a net gain of 190,000 lives saved. Complete termination of the first set of activities is efficient if none of them can save any lives at a cost of less than $80,000 per life saved and if the added $10 billion in the second set of activities uniformly yields other benefits, such as improved health, reduced injuries, and so on, at least equal to such benefits from the first set. As a result, the least efficient activity in the best program has a cost per life saved of $80,000 (where for simplicity we disregard the issue of allocating the cost among various benefits). A straightforward way to assure that the total budget of $20 billion is obtaining the greatest possible results is to use the figure of $80,000 as a criterion for the inclusion and exclusion of particular activities. Any activity or part of an activity costing more than $80,000 per life saved, for this example, should be deleted from the budget, whereas any costing less should be included. If, as a result of this detailed analysis, the total resulting expenditures are less than the available $20 billion, the criterion figure of $80,000 can be raised slightly and activities accordingly added or expanded, until expenditures come up to $20 billion. The resulting criterion value depends on the total budget and the array of possible activities to which it can be devoted. This value, whether $80,000 or higher, is the "value of life" implied by the supposed $20 billion budget, wisely allocated.

Efficiency in the regulation of private sector activities affecting health and safety requires a similar exercise. Although there is no formal "budget" for the upper limit of costs of compliance that can be imposed on private households directly or through increased business costs, there must be a limit to such costs, a limit that is considerably less than the entire net product of the private sector. Good management requires that this limiting amount be recognized and budgeted in a way similar to the budgeting described for government activities. Private health and safety measures required by government regulation should accordingly be evaluated according to a criterion value of cost per life saved. Those measures for which the cost per life saved is higher than the criterion value should not be required. Failure to follow this rule would result in needless loss of life, as in the example of the government programs in which fewer lives were saved at a higher cost per life. If it is assumed that the allowable total of compliance costs imposed on the private sector is fixed and arbitrary, the criterion value of maximum cost per life saved through regulation need not be the same as the criterion value established for government programs. If private compliance costs could be freely substituted for taxation, dollar for dollar, then the two "budgets" could be managed as one, and a single criterion value would result.

The potential for better management is apparent in Table 4, which shows estimated costs of lives saved for several public and publicly supported activities. The lowest estimate in the table is $37,500, once recommended by the National Safety Council as the figure to use in benefit-cost analysis. It is reasonable to suppose that the actual cost per life saved in highway construction and improvement is lower than this figure (after allowing for recent inflation) because most new highways justify their costs through the convenience they provide to motorists. Improved safety is a byproduct, involving very low costs for particular items such as safety barriers. The estimate of $100,000 per life saved through elimination of railroad grade crossings is closer to a pure life-saving estimate, but even that improve-

TABLE 4

SAMPLE ESTIMATES OF THE COST PER LIFE SAVED IN PROGRAMS
SUPPORTED, OPERATED, OR MANDATED BY GOVERNMENT

Program	Cost per Life Saved (dollars)
Medical expenditure[a]	
Kidney transplant	72,000
Dialysis in hospital	270,000
Dialysis at home	99,000
Traffic safety	
Recommended for benefit-cost analysis by the National Safety Council	37,500[a]
Estimate for elimination of all railroad grade crossings	100,000[b]
Military policies[a]	
Instructions to pilots on when to crash-land airplanes	270,000
Decision to produce a special ejector seat in a jet plane	4,500,000
Mandated by regulation	
Coke oven emissions standard, OSHA	4,500,000 to 158,000,000[c]
Proposed lawn mower safety standards, CPSC	240,000 to 1,920,000[d]
Proposed standard for occupational exposure to acrylonitrile, OSHA	1,963,000 to 624,976,000[e]

[a] Dan Usher, "An Imputation to the Measure of Economic Growth for Changes in Life Expectancy," in M. Moss, ed., *The Measurement of Economic and Social Performance* (New York: National Bureau of Economic Research, 1973).

[b] Robert F. Baker, *The Highway Risk Problem* (New York: Wiley, 1971), p. 127.

[c] Statement on behalf of the Council on Wage and Price Stability by Dr. John F. Morrall III before the Occupational Safety and Health Administration, Washington, D.C., May 11, 1976.

[d] Comments of the Council on Wage and Price Stability before Consumer Product Safety Commission (CPSC), August 15, 1977.

[e] Statement on behalf of the Vistron Corporation by James C. Miller III before the Occupational Safety and Health Administration, Washington, D.C., April 4, 1978.

ment involves a nontrivial time-saving convenience for motorists. The figure could also be reduced by concentrating on those grade crossings where the benefit relative to cost is greatest. The other estimates in Table 4 range up to the high of $625 million per life saved, the high end of the range of recognized uncertainty for the proposed occupational health standard for exposure to acrylonitrile, a carcinogen.

The extreme discrepancies in this table indicate dramatic opportunities to save more lives by using resources more effectively. Suppose that OSHA were to adopt a compromise standard for acrylonitrile that, when more reliable data became available, would cost $50 million per life saved. Then a more effective alternative would be to ease this standard enough to save the chemical industry $50 million per year, tax the industry this amount instead, and use the proceeds to improve highway safety. If the first $50 million per year added to highway budgets would eventually eliminate grade crossings, saving an average of one life for each $100,000 spent, the addition would save 500 lives per year on the highways. This compares very favorably with saving only one life per year by forcing the chemical industry to spend $50 million annually to comply with the prospective acrylonitrile standard. Other health and safety standards already proposed or adopted involve hundreds of millions of dollars in prospective annual costs, and more will follow. The resources that are committed, or will be committed, to saving a few lives through these standards could instead save thousands of lives if used as effectively as possible in other programs, according to present evidence.

The underlying reason for the mismanagement implicit in the numbers in Table 4, in the case of health and safety standards, is that the law directs such agencies as OSHA to make workplaces and products as safe as possible with the best available technology. The law says nothing about assuring that compliance costs are reasonable relative to the expected results.[7] Consequently these agencies decide standards mainly in terms of what is feasible and estimate costs and results only to the extent that they are forced to do so by executive order of the president. Nothing in the law calls for a comprehensive strategy to improve health and safety in the most effective possible way subject to a limit on the resources used. Such a strategy would pay large dividends.

---

[7] For a full discussion, see Paul R. Portney, "Toxic Substance Policy and the Protection of Human Health," in P. R. Portney, ed., Current Issues in U.S. Environmental Policy (Washington, D.C.: Resources for the Future, 1978).

3

How Much Is Enough?

The discussion in the previous chapter suggests the question, How much is enough? I have considered effectiveness and the danger of reckless disregard of costs, and effectiveness with a given upper limit on the resources used for life-saving activities. The analysis of benefits and costs can also help decide the proper upper limit on these resources. To analyze efficient management, I will disregard the other political influences that determine budget sizes and suppose that each activity will be expanded or contracted until a small added expenditure would have benefits equal to the expenditure.

In this case, the budget for life-saving activities is not given and fixed but is varied until the criterion value per life saved reaches the right level. Determining this level requires an *independent* estimate of the "value per life saved" from outside the analysis of life-saving activities. For this purpose I will concentrate on the approaches that follow most directly from the earlier discussion of benefit-cost analysis.

Earnings-Based Approaches

It is frequently said that the "value" of a person's life is what he or she will add to the national product, discounted to a present value. If correct, this view would set a relatively low upper limit on the resources that should be devoted to health and safety. Using this value as a criterion for the amounts spent on safety and health activities (duly taking other benefits into account, as well) would mean choosing the level of these activities that leads to the largest measured real national product.[1] This standard of choice may seem appealing,

---

[1] See E. J. Mishan, "Evaluation of Life and Limb," *Journal of Political Economy*, vol. 79 (July/August 1971), p. 687.

but it is inconsistent with what people sometimes choose in the private sector. For example, although it is possible to work sixty or eighty hours a week (and a few people do work that much), most workers prefer the current standard of leisure and work approximately a forty-hour week. In so limiting their work week, they lower their cash incomes and the total national product.

Likewise, in deciding whether to accept risky jobs, to take risky modes of travel, or to engage in risky recreational activities, people perform their own implicit benefit-cost calculations, and there is no presumption that they wish simply to maximize their expected incomes and do not wish to avert risk. On the contrary, the literature on finance and securities shows a wealth of evidence that most investors are risk-averters; hence they invest less in risky investments than would be necessary to maximize real national product. The purchase of life insurance, with nontrivial insurance company costs (so that the expected value of the policy is less than the premiums), shows that the purchasers are risk-averters with respect to the financial aspects of risk of their death. Hence it can be presumed that they are unwilling to take as much personal risk as would be required to maximize real national product. It follows that the discounted present value of a person's contribution to national product—his before-tax earnings and fringe benefits—is smaller than the value implied by the income people sacrifice to obtain greater safety or by the time and effort they devote to safety. This latter value, being higher, means that health and safety yield greater benefits than merely the protection of people's future earnings. Accordingly, it implies that we should spend more to save lives than the discounted future earnings of the persons whose lives we expect to save.

Useful surveys and analyses of a number of other views on this issue have been made by Zeckhauser and Jones-Lee.[2] A curious variant is to consider the value of a person's life to be only his contribution to others—his production minus his consumption discounted for futurity. This measures his value as if he were a slave worth only the profit others make from his efforts and not, himself, a member of the society whose welfare is served by government programs. This variant has even less relation to a willingness to pay for safety than does the discounted value of future earnings. In an extreme case, this approach would count as a positive benefit the death of a retired person who has no future personal earnings but who will continue to consume. Such a concept has no place in an appraisal of the benefits of prolonged life.

[2] Zeckhauser, "Procedures for Valuing Lives"; M. N. Jones-Lee, The Value of Life: An Economic Analysis (Chicago: University of Chicago Press, 1976).

Another variant of the earnings approach adds an amount for pain and suffering, including that of potentially bereaved friends and relatives, to a person's discounted future earnings as an estimate of his "value." This approach comes closer to the notion of willingness to pay, but it still differs in a fundamental respect: it views the problem as one of putting a value on a particular life, whereas the pertinent concept is that of the benefit of an improvement in safety for each of a large number of people.

Court awards of compensatory damages for deaths are irrelevant to benefit-cost analysis for similar reasons. Each award sets a value on the life of a particular person by a procedure that is necessarily arbitrary and subjective. Even if these awards were internally consistent and highly predictable, which is scarcely the case, they represent the wrong concept for use in an appraisal of the benefit of safety.

Willingness to Pay for Safety

Basic to benefit-cost analysis of a project is the notion that benefits and costs to private households can be gauged in most cases by the flow of goods and services associated with the project and valued at market prices. The goods and services that the project consumes—labor, materials, and so on—are costs, whereas the goods and services it creates are benefits. The market price of each good or service measures precisely what households are willing to pay to obtain an incremental unit of each—either the last unit purchased or one additional unit. If the project consumes or creates enough of a good or service to change its price by making it appreciably scarcer or more plentiful, the analyst tries to value each unit at its worth to private households. For example, if an irrigation project adds to the supply of a crop and lowers its market price, the first additional unit of the crop would have sold at approximately the old market price if only that unit had been added, whereas the last additional unit of the crop sells at the new price. If a smaller amount had been added, it would have sold at an intermediate price. The procedure in such a case is to use an average of the old price, the new price, and the intermediate prices; this average will be near the halfway point between the old and the new price.[3] Hence the precise valuation of added quantities supplied or of goods and services consumed depends on the circumstances. Whenever possible, however, this valuation is based on market prices that

---

[3] Edward Renshaw, "A Note on the Measurement of Benefits from Public Investment in Navigation Projects," *American Economic Review*, vol. 47 (September 1957), pp. 652-62.

reflect the values private households place, directly or through business firms, on the affected goods and services.

In some cases costs and benefits must be estimated indirectly or inferred because pertinent market prices do not exist. A new public park seldom has an exact commercial counterpart, so that the amount the public would be willing to pay for its services must be inferred by indirect means, such as by the distances people willingly travel and costs they incur to use such parks.[4] Safety is a benefit (or a reduction in safety a cost) of this type. Only a few items sold in private markets, such as automobile seat belts, serve the sole function of increasing safety. When the installation of seat belts in a new car was optional their purchase provided some information on the public's willingness to pay for safety. However, seat belts also involve a degree of inconvenience, as evidenced by the unwillingness of many people to use them. The added price of inconvenience is hard to measure and must be inferred from indirect evidence.

The most direct evidence of the amount people are willing to pay for their own safety comes from the job market, which offers a variety of working environments with various degrees of personal risk. A worker with a given education and skill level generally can choose among several types of jobs sometimes having markedly different accident rates. A police officer can enter private detective work or become a plant guard, the former safer and the latter more dangerous than regular police work. A lumberjack can take a job in a sawmill, where the work is much safer (and the pay lower). Some workers feel absolutely committed to their narrow specialties, but many are mobile and choose the job they consider most attractive in light of pay, working conditions, risk, and so on. Supply and demand for workers in the various jobs sets wages and wage differentials, including whatever extra wage is necessary to compensate for extra risk. The wage differential for risk will be more than enough for the worker who feels committed to the risky job, whereas it will be too little for the worker who is mobile and is more risk-averse than average. It will be barely adequate to attract some mobile workers in the labor force—those least committed to the risky job and those who would otherwise be willing to accept this job but happen instead to find and accept less risky jobs at lower pay. For such workers, the wage differential precisely measures their willingness to pay for safety.

A further consideration, however, is that the safety of each person affects other persons as well. Many people, perhaps most, are

[4] Marion Clawson, *Methods of Measuring the Demand for and Value of Outdoor Recreation* (Washington, D.C.: Resources for the Future, 1959).

willing to volunteer time and trouble to aid afflicted or threatened persons and to give cash donations to such organizations as the Cancer Society. Market prices of things persons buy for their own safety and wage differentials based on risk contain no information on the amount they would be willing to pay for the safety of *other* persons.[5] We must therefore estimate this factor using reasoning and sketchy, indirect indicators.

Again, information on how people value their own safety is conveyed by the purchase of life insurance. For a representative term life insurance policy, premiums are about 1.6 times the value of claims; that is, to reduce the risk of financial hardship to their beneficiaries, purchasers pay a premium in excess of the payout of claims that they can on average expect to receive. The benefit of this protection is evidently worth at least 1.6 times the amounts paid out by the policies because that is what the policy holders are willing to pay for it. The conclusion would be clear if the face value of a person's term life insurance policy were equal to the discounted present value of his future earnings. A program that would reduce to zero the risk of his death before retirement age would have as its financial benefit for him and his beneficiaries the amount of his insurance premiums, inasmuch as he could cancel the policy. This information by itself strongly suggests that the value of a person's life, based on private decisions, is substantially greater than the discounted present value of his future earnings. Moreover, the program would have the further benefit of keeping the protected persons alive, which insurance does not do. The excess of the value of a life over discounted future earnings is accordingly likely to be even greater than the 1.6 figure implied by the ratio of premiums to claims on term life insurance.

In fact, however, the typical worker has less than one-fourth of the present value of his future earnings covered by life insurance, and just over one-fourth covered by survivors' benefits under social security (see Appendix). We can assume that the worker has a downward-sloping demand curve for life insurance coverage, so that he values the insurance coverage of the first few dollars of his income by more than the last unit of coverage that he buys. That is, in the technical language of benefit-cost analysis, his insurance yields some consumer's surplus. Additional units of coverage, beyond what he buys at 1.6 times the expected value of the policy, would be worth less to him. Thus a policy that would cover his entire income in the event of his death could be worth either more or less than 1.6 times its actuarial value. However, a policy that insured his income in the

---

[5] For an extended discussion, see Mishan, "Evaluation of Life and Limb."

event of his surviving an accident that caused his total disability would presumably be worth more to him than an ordinary term life insurance policy, per unit of expected value, because in this event he, himself, would have to live out of this income, along with his dependents. As just noted, a program that prevents accidents altogether and improves his prospects of being alive and well will be worth substantially more per unit of income-earning capacity protected. How much more can be estimated, can fortunately be checked against several independent pieces of evidence.

Another suggestive line of thought is to note that life consists of more than earning income, which takes about 40 of the 168 hours each week. The hours spent earning income are worth the amount the worker produces (and earns); his leisure hours also have value.[6] When balancing additional income against additional risk, a person can be presumed to require compensation for the risk to both. The extra compensation for risk to the future enjoyment of leisure would be separate from and additional to the necessary compensation for financial risk aversion, where the latter is indicated by the willingness to buy insurance.[7] Hence this reasoning reinforces the thrust of the preceding discussion.

Now consider the arithmetic of compensation for personal risk as it applies to job-market choices. Suppose that we know the precise extra wage that compensates for a known extra risk of death in a job that has no appreciable extra risk of nonfatal injury (a possible example would be airline pilot, engineer, navigator, or stewardess). For a person on the margin of indifference between this job and a less risky one that is otherwise comparable—that is, for a person willing to accept either job—the extra wage is an accurate indicator of his own value of safety. To convert this information into an amount per life lost or per death avoided, divide the extra wage by the extra risk:

$$X = \frac{\text{extra annual wage for the risky job}}{\text{extra annual risk in the risky job}}.$$

For example, if the extra risk is 0.001, that is, one death per year per thousand workers, and if the extra wage for risk is $250 per year, then the ratio is $X = \$250/0.001 = \$250,000$. For the worker indifferent about the two jobs, the extra wage indicates a value of risk avoidance of $250,000 per expected death avoided, by his own market choices. To interpret this number, consider a group of 1,000 such workers who

---

[6] Arnold C. Harberger suggested this point in conversation.

[7] The theory supporting some of the points in these paragraphs is ably set out in Cook and Graham, "The Demand for Insurance and Protection," p. 143.

happen to find and accept safe jobs, though all would have accepted the riskier job had openings been available. In this group, each year one (different) worker on the average will survive who would have suffered a fatal injury had they all been in the risky occupation. In avoiding this one annual death the group has done without a total of $250,000 of annual income—$250 each for 1,000 workers. By assumption, they are on the margin of indifference, so that they would willingly have accepted the extra death and the extra income. Thus the arithmetic of their choice indicates that they consider $250,000 to be the right compensation for one expected death.

In a similar way, if a job has an extra risk of injury without an extra risk of death, the extra pay for that job implies a certain compensation for each expected injury. Dividing the extra pay by the extra risk of injury, indicates the implied compensation per injury. In this case, however, the figure would be an average for injuries ranging from a cut finger to total blindness or loss of several limbs. Whereas all deaths can be said to have the same degree of severity apart from possible differences related to the circumstances of death, the variety of injuries would make this ratio unreliable for application to problems where the relevant severity could differ from that implied in the ratio. A more serious difficulty connected with injuries and ill health is that the job market offers a set of risky jobs with both an extra risk of death and an extra risk of injury. The extra pay for these jobs compensates both risks and, as noted, a wide range of injuries varying in severity is involved.

Estimating willingness to pay for safety from data on seat-belt use is in principle about the same as using data on wage differentials for hazardous jobs. The driver of a car weighs the time lost in fastening his seat belt, plus any inconvenience or annoyance he may feel in wearing the belt, against the reduced risk of death and injury. As in the case of workers choosing jobs, risk avoidance has an implied value of X per death avoided. Similarly, Y is the average value per injury avoided by reducing risk; K is the cost of seat-belt use in time and inconvenience; P is the extra risk of death for the nonuser of a seat belt; and R is the extra risk of injury for the nonuser. The user of a seat belt believes the benefits to exceed the costs, so that $PX + RY \geq K$, whereas for the nonuser $PX + RY \leq K$. If for the average driver we know the values of P, R, Y, and the value of K at which he would be just at the margin of indifference between using and not using his seat belt, we can set the above expressions at equality and rearrange to obtain $X = (K - RY)/P$.

34

The extra risks can be estimated from accident data, and the approximate direct costs of an injury are also known. Where these costs are relatively small, the accuracy or inaccuracy of extra allowances for the desire to avoid pain and suffering and for financial risk aversion will have only a small effect on the accuracy of the resulting estimate of X. Also, the time cost of using a seat belt can be estimated; if this cost is substantially more important to the average driver than any feeling of annoyance or inconvenience and if one can estimate from other behavior the value to a driver of his time, the value of K and the value of the entire above expression for X can be estimated.[8]

The above methods for estimating X give average values for large population groups, but no information about the dependence of X on age, income, and other personal characteristics. They are useful indicators of approximately the right value of X for programs affecting large cross-sectional groups, though not necessarily for special atypical groups.

The use of surveys asking people what they would pay for stated risk reductions is another possible method of estimation sometimes advocated.[9] Although surveys can provide answers to some easily understood questions, such as the relative risk of different jobs (an example is cited in the next section), their usefulness for hypothetical, difficult questions is doubtful. I know of only one published study that used the survey method to estimate willingness to pay for improved safety, and I question the reliability of such surveys.[10] Tentative unpublished experiments with this technique have yielded hopelessly confused and unreliable data. Therefore I concentrate entirely on evidence from actual behavior.

Studies Applying Willingness-to-Pay Concepts

Several studies shed light on the approximate willingness to pay for safety in the United States and on the uncertainties in its estimation.

---

[8] Glenn Blomquist, "Value of Life: Implications of Automobile Seat Belt Use" (Ph.D. dissertation, University of Chicago, 1977). See also his "Value of Life Saving: Implications of Consumption Activity," *Journal of Political Economy*, vol. 87 (June 1979).

[9] For example, see E. J. Mishan, *Cost-Benefit Analysis* (New York: Praeger, 1971); Thomas Schelling, "The Life You Save May Be Your Own," and Martin J. Bailey, "Comment," in Samuel B. Chase, Jr., ed., *Problems in Public Expenditure Analysis* (Washington, D.C.: Brookings Institution, 1968), pp. 163-64.

[10] Jan Paul Acton, "Measuring the Monetary Value of Lifesaving Programs," *Law and Contemporary Problems*, vol. 46 (Autumn 1976), pp. 46-72.

The following review of such studies is not exhaustive but concentrates on those that seem most suggestive and helpful.

Thaler and Rosen Study. One of the earliest and most meticulous attempts to relate wage differentials to risk is a study by Richard Thaler and Sherwin Rosen.[11] They estimated the influences of several variables, including risk, on occupational wage differences. Controlling for the other variables, Thaler and Rosen found a clear systematic tendency for wage rates to rise with increasing risk. The data for the study covered occupational specialties with obvious, easily measured risks, such as lumbering and plant protection. Several estimates of the extra wage to compensate for risk cluster around $200,000 per death in 1967 dollars. This figure sets the upper limit on the value per death that workers in the study sample of risky occupations placed on the extra risk, if the possibility that part of the value may be masked by insurance is disregarded. The workers in the study sample had average earnings of about $6,600 per year in 1967. The average present value of these earnings for all workers, discounted at a rate of 10 percent for the remaining time to retirement, is about $51,500 per worker. If workers do not positively prefer risk, the value they implicitly place on their lives cannot be less than this figure. Hence the actual value implied by these data must lie between $51,500 and $200,000 in 1967 dollars.

The data on occupational hazards and wage differentials, used by Thaler and Rosen, suffer from several problems:

1. Workers in particularly hazardous occupations choose those jobs voluntarily and are therefore less averse to personal hazard than are those who avoid such jobs. Since hazardous jobs represent a small part of total employment, these workers are unrepresentative of the general population. For other persons the benefit of safety is higher.

2. Hazardous jobs include the risks of both death and injury, and the extra wages compensate both risks. There is no fully reliable way to separate the compensation for these two components. Compensation for injury compensates for a wide variety of possible injuries of differing severity.

3. Despite the extra compensation for risk, persons in hazardous jobs have lower incomes than do other workers, mainly because of their lower level of skills. Given the same degree of risk aversion, a

---

11 "The Value of Saving a Life," in Nestor E. Terleckyj, ed., *Household Production and Consumption* (New York: National Bureau of Economic Research, 1976).

high-income person is willing to pay more for safety than a low-income worker.

4. If workers in hazardous jobs carry some life insurance (including that provided by worker's compensation) and if their personal insurance premiums do not rise to cover their added risk, other policy holders bear the cost of their added risk. Others also bear the cost of added risk if the employer pays the premiums for worker's compensation, and the cost of added risk therefore does not appear as cash wage differentials. Similarly, survivors' benefits under social security cover part of the financial risk to dependents without extra charge to workers with high risk. These considerations imply that their extra compensation pays only for their value of survival and *part* of its financial consequences.

The last three of these four problems require appropriate adjustment in the estimates of the value of safety derived from wage differentials for hazardous work. (The first deserves adjustment also, but it is too speculative to attempt.) The adjustments must necessarily be partly arbitrary and approximate because of the lack of adequate supporting data. We know that higher income brings a greater demand for safety; however, the precise relationship between income from various sources and the willingness to pay for safety is unclear. Although dealing with these problems requires subjective adjustments, we can check the result against estimates from other sources.

Consider, for example, the second of these problems. Wage differentials for hazardous jobs reflect the risks of both deaths and injuries. I show in the Appendix that, in terms of compensation that would be required, the type of injury of main concern to a worker in a hazardous job is permanent disablement, and that those permanently disabled typically have to stop working for several years and then take a different job. Since worker's compensation in 1967 covered only a fraction of earnings lost from permanent disablement, the prospect of such an injury, which is more than six times as probable as a fatal injury, must require substantial compensation. I estimate that some 56 percent of the extra compensation for risk compensates for the expectation of injury (with the remaining 44 percent allocated to the risk of death).

I have also adjusted the Thaler-Rosen results for the willingness of general taxpayers to support reduction of workplace hazards because they expect fewer accidental deaths will result in production gains and increases in tax receipts. Further, I have adjusted this result for the expected saving in medical costs that would be borne by third parties. Finally, I have adjusted the numbers to correspond to 1978 prices and incomes. The details of these adjustments are described in the Appendix.

An additional possible consideration is that workers in dangerous jobs could be unaware of the risks or could estimate them with error. A common assumption is that they underestimate risk; however, it is also possible that they overestimate the probability of injury and death. I know from personal experience that in dangerous occupations, such as logging, accidental deaths and injuries are everyday topics of conversation among the workers. For every serious accident there are dozens of minor ones and near misses; the differences in risk among different jobs are therefore easy to perceive and, for those so inclined, easy to exaggerate. It is easy for college graduates and professors to imagine that manual laborers are ignorant in all things, including the risks they face. In fact, there is no reason to suppose that the worker either overestimates or underestimates his job risk, although either is possible. Moreover, it is not the perception of the average worker, or of the average worker in the dangerous job, that matters; it is the perception of workers who consider the wage differential for risk to be barely adequate or not quite enough—those who help determine how much this differential must be—which determines the reliability of the Thaler-Rosen estimates. These workers are the most mobile and have the greatest incentive to evaluate carefully the relative and absolute risks. Both the Thaler-Rosen estimates and survey data are consistent with the presumption that these workers assess the risks consistently and correctly, and I therefore make no adjustment for their possible errors.[12]

The following is a summary of the adjustments I have applied to the Thaler-Rosen estimates, noted above and described in detail in the Appendix.

1. Only about 44 percent of the Thaler-Rosen estimate of X is compensation for the risk of death, the rest being compensation for the risk of injury; hence I adjust the value downward.

2. I adjust the value upward to reflect third-party effects in life insurance and in survivors' benefits of old-age and survivors' insurance (OASI).

3. I adjust the value upward because average worker incomes were higher than the earnings of the workers in the Thaler-Rosen sample.

---

[12] University of Michigan Institute for Social Research, *Survey of Working Conditions*, SRC Study no. 45369 (Ann Arbor: University of Michigan Social Science Archives, 1975). The survey indicates that workers rank jobs approximately accurately by their relative risk.

4. I adjust the value upward to reflect third-party effects through indirect business taxes.

5. I adjust the value upward from 1967 dollars to 1978 dollars.

6. I adjust the value upward to reflect medical costs and other costs of a fatality borne outside the immediate family of the victim.

The cumulative effects of upward adjustments 2 through 6 more than offset the first downward adjustment. The resulting adjusted estimate is $303,000 compared with the Thaler-Rosen figure of $200,000. Since the suggested adjustments to the Thaler-Rosen estimate involve several uncertainties, I have calculated a range of estimates for the corrected and updated value of the compensation for risk of death. In 1978 dollars they are: low, $170,000; intermediate, $303,000; and high, $584,000. Thus willingness to pay, as estimated from the wage differentials analyzed by Thaler and Rosen and as adjusted here, implies a value of safety of several hundred thousand dollars per life saved—perhaps as little as $170,000, perhaps as much as about $600,000.

Blomquist's Estimates. Blomquist's estimates based on the use of automobile seat belts offer a comparison. In addition to the principal estimate he presents, Blomquist showed the variation that results from altering his assumptions, using somewhat different procedures than those I have used for deriving various estimates from the Thaler-Rosen data.

Blomquist used an elaborate, ingenious method of inferring an average value of life from variations in seat belt use associated with thirteen different household characteristics. The basic idea was that using the seat belt takes time, to which the driver attaches a value. Blomquist also considered the possibility that the driver finds use of the seat belt disagreeable. Blomquist used evidence from other studies that the value of a driver's time can be considered to be approximately half his wage, and he found that seat belt use varied in the expected way with the wage, when *lifetime* earnings are held constant. Using wage variation to predict extremes of seat belt use and nonuse, Blomquist derived an implied value of life for which just half of a representative array of drivers would use their seat belts. Blomquist adjusted for injury avoidance as part of the motive for seat belt use, and his estimates depend in part on this adjustment.[13]

---

[13] Blomquist relied on a National Highway Traffic Safety Administration estimate of the average cost (including "pain and suffering") of a traffic injury. If the figure he used ($950) was off by 50 percent, the value of life estimate was dis-

TABLE 5

Blomquist and Thaler-Rosen Estimates of the Value of Life

	Blomquist Estimates			Thaler-Rosen Estimates
	As presented by Blomquist (1975 dollars) (1)	Adusted for inflation only (1978 dollars) (2)	As adjusted by Bailey (1978 dollars) (3)	As adjusted by Bailey (1978 dollars) (4)
Low	142,000	173,000	256,000	170,000
Intermediate	257,000	313,000	409,000	303,000
High	488,000	594,000	715,000	584,000

Sources: (1) Glenn Blomquist, "Value of Life: Implications of Automobile Seat Belt Use" (Ph.D. dissertation, University of Chicago, 1977); (2) first column × 1.218 for increase in consumer price index from 1975 to 1978; (3) (second column × 1.09 [indirect business taxes]) + $14,400 (third-party medical costs) + $53,000 (third-party insurance effect), as explained in text; and (4) Appendix.

His estimate, along with his highest and lowest estimates for alternative assumptions, are shown in Table 5. The first column shows Blomquist's estimates as he presented them. In the second these numbers are adjusted upward by 22 percent for inflation from 1975 to 1978. In the third, indirect business taxes, third-party medical costs, and third-party insurance effects in 1978 dollars are added as for the estimates derived from Thaler and Rosen that are reported in the fourth column. The third-party insurance effect is larger, after adjustment to 1978 dollars, than the corresponding figure for the Thaler-Rosen estimates because there is no allowance in life insurance premiums for the insured's habits with regard to seat belt use.

The two arrays of estimates, those derived from Thaler and Rosen and those derived from Blomquist, agree fairly well. The Blomquist

placed by less than 5 percent, so that its importance is small. One reason for this small effect, compared to the larger adjustment that I have made for the Thaler-Rosen estimates, is that he finds that protection from injuries provides only a small share (about 10 percent) of the benefit from using seat belts. This small share results mainly from evidence that seat belts are less effective in preventing injuries than in preventing deaths. Therefore, most of the benefit of using seat belts is in preventing deaths rather than in preventing injuries. The ratio of injuries to deaths in automobile accidents may also differ from that in industrial accidents, although there is little evidence on this point. See Blomquist, "Value of Life Saving: Implications of Consumption Activity," *Journal of Political Economy*, vol. 87 (June 1979).

estimates are roughly $100,000 higher than the Thaler-Rosen estimates. One possible reason for this difference is self-selection of workers in hazardous jobs, with the result that workers in these hazardous jobs accept risks with lower compensation than would be required by people in the population cross-section studied in the Blomquist data. However, the main point to be noted in Table 5 is the broad agreement in estimates to which a consistent set of adjustments was applied, even though the estimates were obtained by two different approaches.

Smith's Estimates. Estimates based on wage differentials are also reported in a study by Robert S. Smith; these estimates suggest much larger compensation for risk.[14] Estimates based on Smith's study are shown in Table 6.

Although these estimates are far larger than those derived from Thaler and Rosen and from Blomquist, ranging up to $2.5 million, the difference can be partly explained by the fact that Smith made no adjustment for compensation for injury. When he attempted to estimate such an adjustment by using injury rates as a variable in his analysis no statistically significant effects were found. He defended this result by arguing that the costs of injuries are fully compensated by worker's compensation payments. My analysis suggests, however, that the compensation for permanent disablement falls short of full compensation. In order to allow comparison, I have adjusted Smith's estimates by allocating to compensation for the expectation of injury the same portion of the extra pay for risk as I did in adjusting the Thaler-Rosen estimates. The adjusted figures are shown in the second column of Table 6. This adjustment brings the estimate for manufacturing within the upper end of the range reported for the Blomquist estimates, but the estimate for all industries remains outside this range and further adjustments are necessary for comparison with the range of adjusted estimates reported in Table 5. If the Smith estimates were adjusted to reflect the value of the dollar in 1978, both estimates would fall well outside the range for the two studies discussed earlier.

---

[14] Robert S. Smith, "The Feasibility of an 'Injury Tax' Approach to Occupational Safety," *Law and Contemporary Problems*, vol. 38 (Summer-Autumn 1974), p. 730. See also his *Occupational Safety and Health Act* (Washington, D.C.: American Enterprise Institute, 1976), appendix B. Omitted from this review is the paper by James R. Chelius, "The Control of Industrial Accidents: Economic Theory and Empirical Evidence," *Law and Contemporary Problems*, vol. 38 (Summer 1974), pp. 700-29. Chelius tried to estimate several relationships simultaneously, including the effect of injury rates on wage differentials. His data were poorly suited to this purpose, and he found no relationship.

TABLE 6
Smith Estimates of the Value of Life and Adjusted Estimates
(dollars)

	Smith Estimates (1)	Adjusted for Expected Injuries (2)
1967, all industries (1967 dollars)	2,500,000	1,100,000
1973, manufacturing (1973 dollars)	1,500,000	600,000

Sources: (1) Robert S. Smith, "The Feasibility of an 'Injury Tax' Approach to Occupational Safety," *Law and Contemporary Problems* (Summer-Autumn 1974), p. 730; (2) adapted from first column using the intermediate value of *S* (that is, *X/Y*) from the Appendix.

While Thaler and Rosen used a sample of workers whose job risks were especially high and for which risk information was reported for detailed occupational categories, Smith used representative samples of workers from all industries taken together and from manufacturing industries, with job risks reported only for industry averages. Hence, the wage differentials were smaller and masked, because they were averages, a great deal of variation among occupational categories. Smith made the occupation of each worker a control variable, so that under his method it is not possible to distinguish between a component of high wages that might be due to the riskiness of an occupation and the part of wages that should be attributed to other characteristics of workers in the occupation itself.

Smith's estimates are not easily reconciled with the Thaler-Rosen estimates by reference only to the most apparent differences in their data and estimation methods. The use of industry wage and risk information, averaged across occupations, and the use of occupations for control variables are possible sources of bias in the Smith estimates. To the extent that the resulting estimates were affected by this aspect of Smith's method, downward bias would be expected and the size of the wage premium for risk implied by Smith's estimates would be even larger.

There may be other factors as well that are obscured by the high level of aggregation. The difference between Smith's "all industries" estimate, for example, and his "manufacturing" estimate would be increased even further if the figures were adjusted for inflation. The large discrepancy in these two estimates, which were obtained using the same assumptions and methods (where, by contrast, the range in

Table 5 reflects different assumptions and methods), suggests that estimates obtained from aggregated data are subject to a very wide range of uncertainty.

Viscusi's Estimates. Another set of estimates based on wage differentials appears in an analysis by Viscusi.[15] Like Smith, he used a sample of workers from several industries; he included occupation and other characteristics of workers as variables; and he used average measures of risk in a given industry as the explanatory variable for estimating the wage premiums attributable to differences in risks. Unlike Smith, he estimated a separate wage premium for the risk of nonfatal injury. His estimates for the value of life ranged from $600,000 to $1,769,500 in 1969–1970 dollars. (In 1978 dollars, they range from about $1,050,000 to $3,250,000.) Differences among the estimates result from the use of alternative and parallel risk variables and from the choice between logarithms and natural numbers for earnings. Like Smith's estimates, Viscusi's are well above the range encompassed by those derived from Thaler and Rosen and from Blomquist when a consistent set of adjustments is applied.

The similarities between Viscusi's and Smith's data and analyses entail similar possible biases. Viscusi argues that his results are representative for the general population and that the Thaler-Rosen estimates represent only those self-selected workers who are least averse to risk. This possibility must be conceded. However, the implied difference in compensation for increased risk of death among workers choosing different occupations would be very large. Moreover, estimates from recent work by Dillingham (discussed in the next section) suggest that broad aggregation levels and difficulties in identifying wage premiums attributable to occupational risk contribute decisively to the difference between the size of estimates obtained by Viscusi and Smith and the size obtained in the Thaler-Rosen and Blomquist studies.

Dillingham's Estimates. A recent analysis by Dillingham provides some insight into these discrepancies.[16] Dillingham used a cross-section of workers for which the data were similar to those used in the Smith and Viscusi studies. In addition, Dillingham obtained detailed risk data by industry and occupation, so that he could assign the workers

---

[15] W. Kip Viscusi, "Labor Market Valuations of Life and Limb: Empirical Evidence and Policy Implications," *Public Policy*, vol. 26 (Summer 1978), pp. 359-86.
[16] Alan E. Dillingham, "The Injury Risk Structure of Occupations and Wages," (unpublished Ph.D. dissertation, Cornell University, 1979), chapter 4.

TABLE 7

Dillingham Estimates of the Value of Life

	Not Adjusted for Injury Risk (1969 dollars)	Adjusted for Injury Risk (1969 dollars)	Adjusted for Inflation[a] (1978 dollars)	As Adjusted by Bailey[b] (1978 dollars)
Blue-collar workers only	368,000	168,000	300,000	376,000
Full-sample of workers[c]	458,000	—	—	—

[a] Based on estimate adjusted for injury risk (column 2).

[b] $300,000 × 1.09 + $14,400 + $35,000. The life insurance plus social security adjustment of $35,000 is $17,000 × 2.05 (see Appendix).

[c] Injury risk was included in several of Dillingham's regressions. Its effect was statistically insignificant in the full cross-section.

in his sample to more detailed risk categories than those used in the other studies. Dillingham grouped his sample of workers into three broad skill categories, but he did not use occupations as control variables. Although his analysis was applied to a different sample of workers, the results from his method help to clear up some of the issues that have been discussed in connection with Smith's and Viscusi's methods.

Dillingham's estimates of the value of life are reported in Table 7. When his estimate for risk of injury is taken into account, and when other adjustments necessary for a consistent comparison with the Thaler-Rosen and Blomquist estimates have been made, an estimate of $376,000 is obtained. This estimate falls near the center of the range of adjusted estimates reported in Table 5. This result suggests that differences in risk aversion in different parts of the population are not the major source of uncertainty, inasmuch as the Dillingham sample includes a broad cross-section of workers whose aversion to risk should be fairly representative. Larger uncertainties seem to arise from other factors.

Dillingham's analysis represents a refinement to the methods and data used by Smith and by Viscusi. The consistency of Dillingham's estimates with the range of those reported in Table 5 supports the idea that more reliance should be placed on the values in this range than on the much higher range represented by the Smith and Viscusi estimates. Although there are many reasons for legitimate doubt about the reliability of this range of estimated values, I will place most of my emphasis on the estimates reported in Table 5. To decide whether this emphasis is justified, we should translate the results into everyday experience. We need some way to get an intuitive feel for the reasonableness of estimates in this range.

Are the Results Reasonable?

Let us consider what these numbers imply. Suppose that the representative family of four with an income of $18,500 in 1978 had an option to purchase a share in a health and safety program that would reduce the average annual risk of death for every member of the family from, say, 6 per thousand to 5.5 per thousand. This improvement is about the same as the drop in death rates that occurred from 1970 to 1975; it is about half the risk difference between the average job and the typical hazardous job. In Table 8, column 1, we have the range of estimates that I judge to be most reliable, those based on analyses by Thaler and Rosen, Blomquist, and Dillingham. The lowest adjusted figure is from the Thaler and Rosen study, the highest from Blomquist, and the intermediate figure from both these sources and from the Dillingham study. Each of the values in column 1 implies an amount the family would be willing to pay for a reduction of the magnitude assumed above in all family members' risk; this amount appears in column 2.

The low figure of $300 is 1.6 percent of family income, the intermediate figure of $700 is 3.8 percent, and $1,400 is about 7.6 percent. Each individual family may differ in its willingness to purchase this improvement in family-member survival; however, the range of 1.6 to 7.6 percent of income, with an intermediate value of 3.8 percent, appears reasonable.

For comparison, a highly advertised home burglar-alarm system costs from $1,000 to $1,500 per year, and the typical smoke-detector system costs less than $100 a year. There are nonnegligible sales of both types of systems, although the majority of households buys neither. The safety improvement they afford is much less than the improvement of 0.5 in deaths per thousand under discussion here, which is equivalent to the elimination of all accidental deaths or the reduction of cancer deaths by one-third. It must be recognized, of course, that such alarm systems would presumably contribute to reduced property losses in addition to their contribution to reduced risks to life.

Now consider what is implied by the higher estimates of the value of life derived from the studies by Smith and Viscusi, ranging

45

TABLE 8

IMPLIED WILLINGNESS OF A FAMILY OF FOUR TO PAY
FOR A HEALTH AND SAFETY PROGRAM
(dollars)

	Value of Life (1)	Willing to Pay (per year) (2)
Low	170,000	300
Intermediate	360,000	700
High	715,000	1,400

NOTE: It is assumed that the program would reduce the death rate from 0.006 to 0.0055.

SOURCES: (1) Appendix; (2) first column × reduction in risk (that is, 0.006 − 0.0055) × number of family members, rounded to the nearest hundred.

up to $2.5 million. In 1978 dollars this high figure becomes $5 million. Using the same formula as that used for column 2 in Table 7, this estimate would imply that the family with average income would be willing to pay $10,000 per year for the stated improvement in family survival, or about 55 percent of family income. This estimate seems to me to be unquestionably too high. New studies will surely come along, however, to improve our estimates and our understanding of this issue.

Policy Concerning Rescue Operations

Many observers have noted that most people are willing to spend more to rescue a lost or trapped person than to avoid a "statistical" death, that is, to avoid some predictable death, say, by a traffic accident or cancer, of someone whose identity is not known. This phenomenon is often regarded as a paradox, although the total amount of resources expended on such rescues is comparatively small.

While almost everyone feels strongly about the importance of trying to save a trapped or lost person, they may not have this same feeling about avoiding future traffic accidents or other causes of death. In a search or rescue operation, there is something tangible and specific that can be done to enhance the chance of survival of an identified victim. We almost all share vicariously in the drama of a rescue, and we would almost all feel guilty if there were no strenuous effort to conduct such a rescue operation.

However, most volunteers in search and rescue operations use time that would otherwise be idle, and the same is likely to be true of equipment. When Air Force squadrons go in search of a downed flier, they use flying time that would be used otherwise for routine practice, unless the budget is increased for this search. It is easy, therefore, to exaggerate the "cost" of search and rescue. The fact remains, however, that the resources used are not valueless, and there is an apparently greater willingness to volunteer resources for this purpose than for almost any other comparable demand. What does this imply for policy?

I see no particular reason for a specific policy regarding voluntary search and rescue efforts or use of idle public resources for this purpose. Policy usefulness arises when advance budgetary commitments are made for search and rescue activities; at that time these operations are on a par with other programs that will save unnamed future individuals. A fire department is designed and funded with a view to saving "statistical" lives and property, as is any other program mainly concerned with rescue. A policy maker or a member of the general public has no reason to use a different value of X for evaluating and choosing the size of such a program than for any other program designed to save lives. However, the level of voluntary efforts and changes in this level in response to government programs may shed light on the appropriate value of X, a point discussed further in the Appendix.

4
Conclusion

The introductory discussion in Chapter 1 noted a paradox in the declining death rates from most causes, cancer being the most notable exception, combined with recent legislation granting sweeping regulatory powers to the federal government over workplace health and safety, environmental pollution, and consumer product safety. For the most part, there is little reason to suppose that such regulation can achieve a significant reduction in deaths from accidents or ill health, with the possible major exception of cancer deaths related to industrial chemicals, smoke, fumes, food additives, and so on. The costs of compliance with such regulation threaten to produce a major reduction in our standard of living and in our rate of economic growth. A coherent and rational discipline can help to limit these costs and to obtain an efficient balance between costs and benefits.

Although efficient use of government resources devoted to health and safety and of private resources mandated by health, safety, and environmental regulations can never be perfectly achieved within our political system, laws can be changed and egregious waste reduced. I have avoided discussion of the political barriers to efficient management of these resources, concentrating instead on the lives lost and the other unnecessary costs incurred when these barriers or simple carelessness seriously interfere with efficiency. I then addressed the question of how to improve efficiency in the use of resources for health and safety, with particular emphasis on the use of a value representing the benefit of saving a life. The proposal to use such a value meets great resistance; opponents seem to view its use as an obstacle to programs to improve health and safety. The real obstacle to these programs is that the resources they require are limited by our political system. These limits, however chosen, unavoidably imply a presumptive benefit per life saved for each program represented by the highest cost per life saved among all elements of the program. Failure to use an explicit value X to help determine the resource limit for each program inevitably lowers the efficiency of the entire set of programs. Pursuing programs in an arbitrary order based on visibility or administrative convenience, regardless of cost, until the total costs reach the limit the public will accept has resulted in extreme disparities in the implied benefit per life saved. These disparities mean that lives are needlessly lost because high-cost, low-benefit programs absorb resources that could otherwise be used for low-cost, high-benefit programs.

A well-considered value X can also play a constructive role in determining the total resources devoted to programs to improve health and safety. In these programs, as in others, the government increases the welfare of its constituents, taken together, when it adopts programs in which benefits exceed costs. Programs in which benefits are less than costs can always be replaced by more efficient substitutes that are preferable for the whole population. Applying the criterion that benefits shall at least equal costs requires the use of a measure of X derived from evidence on the amount private households are willing to pay for improved safety and greater life expectancies.

I have presented estimates based on five studies of the amounts a large group of persons of average tastes and income and a cross-section of ages would be willing to spend per life saved to reduce their exposure to mortal risk. These estimates are scarcely definitive, as the stated range of uncertainty has an upper limit three times the lower limit; indeed, the uncertainty may be even greater than that. Future research can be expected to narrow this range and could possibly lead to a value outside the stated range. The point of presenting these estimates is to show that reasonable estimates can be derived from evidence on household and worker behavior and to show some of the issues involved.

When the uncertainties are narrowed, policy makers can move with greater confidence toward making small adjustments to the average figures for programs affecting special target populations. Risk level, income, age, and other factors might differ from the average in such a population, and these factors imply different values of X, based on choices made by groups that match the target group.

It is possible that evidence on worker choices between jobs of different risk is irrelevant to the problem because workers may not correctly estimate the risks. Although the evidence cited is internally consistent and gives no indication of worker error in this respect, it is also consistent with systematic worker error in estimating this risk. Unfortunately, in the work of experts who operate government programs affecting health and safety, there is clear evidence both of inconsistency and of systematic error. Huge differences in the cost per life saved in different programs represent inconsistency; the use of discounted values of future earnings of workers alone for X represents systematic underestimation. The performance of experts gives no basis for confidence that their opinions should supersede the evidence of household and worker behavior in the marketplace. This evidence, even in the present early stage of study, implies uncertainties which are narrower than the range of choices by experts.

The results presented here indicate that existing government programs for health and safety will save more lives if officials use good estimates of benefits and costs to guide each program decision. It appears also that some programs would be less ambitious and some more ambitious than at present with the use of such estimates. I cannot judge what the overall total of resources committed to health and safety would be nor how this total would compare with the present level of effort.

At present the president requires regulatory agencies within his administration to estimate costs and benefits of their proposed regulations; he also requires such estimates for proposed spending programs. Independent regulatory bodies, such as the Consumer Product Safety Commission or the Federal Aviation Administration, are not required to consider costs and benefits explicitly. For those agencies that do undertake benefit-cost analysis, there are no uniform standards nor requirements that the agencies take the estimation seriously. These deficiencies could be remedied, and the influence of political pressures and bias could perhaps be reduced with changes like the following:

- Extend the requirement for benefit-cost analysis to all relevant agencies, including autonomous regulatory agencies.
- Establish and enforce high standards of quality and reliability for this analysis. (The natural agency to perform this function would be the Office of Management and Budget.)
- Publish timely benefit-cost analyses of agency proposals and of principal alternatives, so that these analyses can receive outside criticism and review before final policy decisions are made.

These procedural changes deal with specific problems discussed above in Chapters 1 and 2. There are other possibilities as well.

Policies such as effluent charges for sources of air and water pollution are one possibility. Using these charges to obtain efficient outcomes would require that the regulatory agency estimate the benefit per ton of reduced emissions—that is, the damage done by the last increment of emissions. The agency need not estimate the cost of control: each firm (or other source of pollution) would decide for itself whether it is costlier to pay the effluent charge or to reduce emissions. Thus half the effort of benefit-cost analysis would devolve upon the firm, whose owners' best interests dictate accurate cost estimates. Such charges or taxes might also be applied to workplace hazards wherever the hazards are not reflected in the employer's premiums for workers' compensation insurance, and where poor knowledge of the hazards (such as suspected carcinogens) may mean that the wage fails to compensate for them.

Another possibility, illuminated by the discussion in Chapter 2, would be to give each regulatory agency a specified "budget" or upper limit for the costs it could impose on the private sector. This upper limit could be revised from year to year in the light of benefit-cost analysis of its regulatory program and of its next options for regulation if the limit were relaxed. Such a rule would encourage a full flow of information from the regulatory agency, from regulated industries, and from other interested parties. It would thus help assure the high quality of cost and benefit estimates that my other suggestions aim for.[17] Appropriate enabling legislation would be required for some of these changes. If enacted and enforced, they could produce striking improvements in the efficiency of programs aimed at better health and safety for Americans.

---

[17] This approach and its advantages were mentioned in a speech by Barry Bosworth, director of the Council on Wage and Price Stability, before a conference in Williamsburg, Virginia, sponsored by the American Council of Life Insurance, February 22, 1979.

APPENDIX

The text noted that the present value of a worker's future earnings averaged some $51,500 in the Thaler-Rosen data. This sets a plausible lower limit for the compensation per death that risk-averse workers require for the risk of death, based on *a priori* reasoning. The Thaler-Rosen estimates using wage differentials for risk set an approximate upper limit on this compensation at $200,000, if none of the compensation is for injuries and if the worker and his family bear all the risk. I now attempt to narrow and adjust this range of uncertainty.

Within this range, the location of the appropriate value depends on several factors, including the share for risk of injury, insurance considerations, indirect business taxes, increases in the price level, and others. The first such factor considered here is the risk of injury. Attempts by Thaler and Rosen and by Dillingham to estimate econometrically how much of the wage differentials are due to the risk of injury and how much to the risk of death have proved unproductive.[1] Therefore, the shares must be estimated indirectly.

The part of the Thaler-Rosen figure that can be allocated to expected injuries depends on the perceived seriousness of an injury compared with a death (in terms of necessary compensation), on the comparative frequencies, and on compensation of victims and their families. To begin, consider the following data from the National Safety Council: In 1975, work-related casualties resulted in 12,600 deaths, 80,000 permanent impairments, and 2,100,000 temporary total disablements. Indications are that temporary total disablements are minor enough to be disregarded. The Bureau of Labor Statistics publishes data suggesting that the average time lost in nonfatal lost-workday accidents is about fifteen days. The costs of an accident of

---

[1] Stated to this author in private conversation.

this severity are reasonably fully covered by sick pay and other fringe benefits necessitating little compensation in the basic wage. Moreover, the cumulative impact of temporary disablements is considerably smaller than that of permanent impairments. Suppose that all lost workdays reported by the Bureau of Labor Statistics were associated with temporary total disablements—that permanent impairments were accounted for in some other way than lost workdays. If so, temporary total disablements at an average length of fifteen days would account for about 31.5 million lost workdays. In contrast, data shown in Table 9 indicate that the representative permanent impairment costs about five years of inability to work, or more than 1,750 workdays per impairment. Therefore, the 80,000 permanent impairments in 1975 imply a total of 140 million days lost from work, or more than four times as many lost days as those due to temporary disablements. These losses are quite serious for the affected workers, involving permanent handicaps and extended periods of pain and suffering. For various reasons it is reasonable to suppose that the prospect of temporary disablements receives little weight in a worker's appraisal of the disadvantages of a job compared with the risk of permanent disablement. Hence it is safe to assume that the compensation required in the wage to cover injuries in 1967 was almost entirely attributed to the prospect of permanent disablements.

In the analysis of the allocation of the wage differential that follows it is assumed that the entire compensation for the risk of death or injury is paid as wages to healthy workers. Disregarded are worker's compensation payments and disability insurance payments (by social security) to injured workers, and survivors' benefits and life insurance paid to the family of a worker killed on the job. The fraction of the worker's earnings replaced by all such payments in 1967 was about the same for a worker with two children whether he was disabled or killed. Therefore the wage compensation to healthy workers required for either of these risks would be reduced in a similar way by the existence of such payments. The allocation of the wage premium between the two risks would be little affected; hence the allocation that applies if there are no such payments is also approximately correct when there are such payments. (After allocating the wage premium between the two risks, I adjust X, derived from the portion attributed to the risk of death, to reflect survivors' benefits and life insurance.)

The symbol X, as before, represents the extra compensation required per expected death, and Y represents the extra compensation required per expected permanent disablement. That is,

$$Y = \frac{\text{extra annual wage for extra risk of permanent injury in the risky job}}{\text{extra annual risk of permanent injury in the risky job}}.$$

This expression represents the total extra wage required by workers to compensate for one expected permanent disablement, exclusive of the compensation for the risk of death. Lacking detailed data, I assume that occupational deaths and permanent injuries in the especially hazardous occupations studied by Thaler and Rosen occur in the same proportions as they do in the working population as a whole. For the entire work force, the total extra compensation for these hazards in 1975 would be $12{,}600X + 80{,}000Y$, and the share attributed to the risk of death (S) would be

$$S = \frac{12{,}600X}{12{,}600X + 80{,}000Y}.$$

If the value of X were known, the Thaler-Rosen figure could be used to calculate S directly, with the equivalent formula $S = X/\$200{,}000$. As noted earlier, if injuries require no compensation, so that $Y = 0$, then $X = \$200{,}000$ and $S = 1$. At the other extreme, if X is merely the discounted present value of future earnings, the Thaler-Rosen data would imply $S = \$51{,}500/\$200{,}000 = 0.26$. If so, the formula for S implies that

$$Y = \frac{0.74(12{,}600)}{0.26(80{,}000)} X = 0.448\, X \; (= \$23{,}100).$$

That is, we have the bounds for Y of $0 \leq Y \leq 0.448\, X$. At the higher bound, a given risk of a permanent impairment requires about 45 percent as much compensation as the same risk of death; that is, $Y/X = 0.448$.

To locate Y within these bounds, and so to determine the share S, we must consider how serious a permanent impairment is. Although information on the duration and severity of permanent impairments does not indicate the required compensation for the risk of such impairment, it can help us make a subjective estimate.

Only indirect information on severity is available. A worker in the labor force from age eighteen to age sixty-five has a roughly constant exposure to risk throughout his working life, although young males under twenty-five have higher accident rates both on the job and elsewhere. A worker who has a serious accident suffers the injury on the average at around age forty-one, when he has twenty-four working years remaining, during which a permanent impairment will limit his ability to work and earn income.

To estimate the extent of an injured worker's handicap, I use data on the distribution of disabilities in the working-age population, provided by a survey conducted by the Social Security Administration in 1966. Inasmuch as almost all on-the-job injuries up to that time involved male workers, I concentrate on the males. Since the survey data include persons temporarily disabled, I have adjusted the data by making rough estimates of the numbers with temporary disabilities in order to obtain estimates of the numbers of disabled males in 1966 for each category of severity (see Table 9). Although these disabilities result both from job-related accidents and from other causes, there is no reason to fear any grossly misleading bias in the percentages because of the inclusion of non-job-related disabilities.

The disabled males in this group acquired their disabilities over the previous several decades. Presumably the most severely disabled are more likely to die prematurely, and their deaths often would not be classified as "occupational"; if so, these data understate the actual severity. It is assumed that all permanently disabled male workers who survived until 1966 are included in the above table. It is also assumed that a permanently disabled worker can expect to remain in one of the three categories in Table 9 for the rest of his working life although, as noted, this assumption underestimates severity. However, there is a possible offsetting error associated with the age structure in a growing population for which I have not attempted to correct. On the average, a worker who suffers a permanent disablement can expect to spend the same percentages of his remaining working life in each of the three categories as the percentages given in Table 9 for the population. For an average remaining time to retirement of twenty-four years at the time of disablement, the periods of disablement work out as shown in column (3) rounded to the nearest integer. In addition, the worker would continue his disability into retirement.

To fix the values of X and Y, we need an estimate of how the compensation required to induce a worker to accept, say, a 0.001 per year risk of permanent disability compares with the compensation required to induce this worker to accept a 0.001 per year risk of death. Accidental death for the average case costs twenty-four years of income, family responsibility, and recreation during the working life, plus the enjoyment of retirement. Permanent disablement for the average case entails five years of inability to work plus the remaining years of partial disability. Surely a given risk of permanent disablement, with this pattern, would require less than 45 percent of the

TABLE 9

ESTIMATED WORKING-AGE MALE PERMANENTLY DISABLED POPULATION,
1966, AND ESTIMATED YEARS OF DISABILITY

(ages 18-64)

Severity of Disability	Number (millions) (1)	Percent (2)	Estimated Years of Disability (3)
Severe[a]	1.4	20	5
Occupational[b]	2.1	30	7
Secondary work limitations[c]	3.5	50	12
Total	7.0	100	24

[a] Defined as unable to work altogether or unable to work regularly.

[b] Defined as able to work regularly, but unable to do the same work as before onset of disability, or unable to work full time.

[c] Defined as able to work full time, regularly, and at the same work as before, but with limitations in the kind or amount of work performed.

SOURCES: (1) and (2) estimated on basis of Social Security Administration, *1966 Social Security Survey of the Disabled*; (3) based on (1) and (2) and the assumption of a uniform distribution of accidents by age of worker.

compensation required for the same risk of death. If so, Y is below the stated upper bound. The conclusion can be justified in other ways than simply the *prima facie* presumption that 45 percent looks too large. If Y were at this bound, it would mean that the worker just barely willing to accept the risky job has no financial risk aversion nor any aversion to death apart from its financial consequence. That is, at this bound X = \$51,500, the discounted 1967 value of the worker's future earnings. Such a worker, to be consistent, would also have to care only about the money in case of an injury and have no risk aversion to permanent disablement. I disregard medical costs, which are generally covered by third parties (health insurance, worker's compensation insurance, and the like). In this case, the logical compensation required for expected injuries would be simply the expected loss of wages, which by the data in Table 9 must surely be less than 45 percent of the wage loss caused by death.

Moreover, if these workers (barely willing to accept the risky job) carry life insurance, as nearly all workers do, they have some risk aversion. That, in turn, implies a higher X and therefore a lower Y, given the fixed $200,000 figure from Thaler and Rosen. If we take as a minimum for X, 1.6 times the discounted value of future earnings, as implied by the discussion of life insurance, $X = \$82,400$. To proceed further, in 1967 the expected survivors' benefits under social security had a discounted value of about $13,000, so that the net X to be provided by extra advance wages would be about $69,000. This value implies a value of 0.3 for Y/X if it is assumed that the part of future wages made good by social security is the same for the disabled worker as for one who dies. Thus, the value 0.3 is a plausible upper limit for Y/X, and $69,000 a plausible lower limit for X in terms of advance wage compensation. Even this figure is too low, however, because it allows nothing for aversion to death.

At the other extreme, the advance wage compensation required for the risk of permanent disability must be well above zero, the value which corresponds to $S = 1$, or $X = \$200,000$. On the basis of the data in Table 9, I conclude that it is unlikely that this compensation could be less than 0.1 times the compensation for an equal extra risk of death. A reasonable intermediate figure would be 0.2; for this figure, if an extra risk of death of 0.001 per year required extra wage compensation of $100 per year, then an extra risk of permanent disablement of 0.001 would require extra wage compensation of $20 per year.

Consider once again the formula for the ratio S:

$$S = \frac{12,600X}{12,600X + 80,000Y}.$$

The intermediate value just obtained for the ratio of Y to X, namely, $Y/X = 0.2$, is rearranged to get $Y = 0.2X$. Substituting this value for Y into the formula for S gives the result

$$S = \frac{12,600X}{12,600X + 80,000(0.2X)} = \frac{12,600}{12,600 + 16,000} = 0.44.$$

Applying this fraction to the Thaler-Rosen estimate to obtain the part attributable to the risk of death, gives

$$X = 0.44\ (\$200,000) = \$88,000.$$

Proceeding in the same way for other trial values of the ratio Y/X, we have the following possible values of X implied by the Thaler-Rosen data:

Y/X	X
0.1	$122,000
0.2	$ 88,000
0.3	$ 69,000

Inasmuch as the estimates of X by Blomquist and by Dillingham point to a value of X roughly in line with the middle case, I will rely mainly on this value for further discussion while keeping the range of uncertainty in mind.

A straightforward way to adjust for the income difference between high-risk and all workers is to multiply a value of X based on the Thaler-Rosen sample by the ratio of national income per worker to the Thaler-Rosen earnings figure of $6,600 per worker. In so doing, the distinction between labor income and property income is ignored. Propertied people might be expected to have greater risk aversion than do workers without property; however, property income is not lost when its owner dies. Because safety is a "luxury," adding property income to earned income should add more than proportionately to the amount spent for safety, except that there is no need to insure the property income itself against personal hazard. Inasmuch as property income is only about one-fifth of total national income, the error from viewing it in the same way as earned income is unlikely to be large. For 1967, the national income per worker is $8,089, the Thaler-Rosen worker income is $6,600, with a ratio of 1.23.

Benefits to Other Persons

The review of evidence up to this point has mainly concerned the benefits of safety to the persons directly protected. In addition, there are benefits to other persons, both directly through their concern for the safety of others and indirectly through financial effects. Evidence of direct concern is the voluntary contributions people make to research organizations concerned with health and safety. Also, people volunteer to help rescue a child trapped in a well and to help in other rescues. However, on this latter point, volunteering or giving cash to save a trapped person must be distinguished from giving time or money to improve health or safety for potential "statistical" victims whose identities are unknown. The sums contributed to research, hospitals, and so on are unimpressive: for 1973, the private charitable giving to health programs and hospitals was reported in *Statistical Abstract of the United States* as just under $4 billion, which was less than half of 1 percent of the national income. It is hard to imagine persons giving voluntarily to street improvements that would add to traffic safety or to the fireproofing of their neighbors' homes.

In most discussions of the benefits of safety to other persons, the "others" referred to are usually the members of the immediate family of the potential victim of tragedy. Members of the immediate family are indeed willing to sacrifice income to increase the survival chances of other members of the family. However, the family is best thought of as having a single combined income. The safety of each of its members has an X value that takes into account the entire willingness to pay for safety out of family income; that is, X for one member includes the benefits of that member's safety to other members of the family. If the primary earner is in a dangerous job with a wage differential that just barely compensates him for his own personal concern for his safety without regard to the concern of the other members of the family, and if they are willing to give up something extra to have him move to a less dangerous job, the family as a whole is less than fully compensated for his risk. In this case, recognition of family concerns will lead him to shift to a less dangerous job. A worker who remains in a dangerous job must be presumed to receive enough extra compensation to cover the risk felt by all members of his family.

Two forms of giving for the health and safety of other persons deserve further consideration. First, some persons serve in volunteer fire departments, serve without pay as school crossing guards, and engage in other similar activities. Second, some of these activities are supported by tax money but would be partly supported by voluntary contributions if the public sector did not fund them.[2] It is possible that the public's willingness to give to such activities and to acquiesce in tax-supported programs reflects a willingness to pay for the benefit of persons outside the family.

Volunteer activities are hard to appraise in dollar terms, and it is difficult to assess the motivation for them. Does the volunteer fireman serve in order to reduce risks to all his neighbors, or does he serve in order to participate in the rescue of life and property at the time of a fire? If the primary objective is to reduce risks, it would be more practical to support a professional fire department. If, as seems likely, a sense of participation is more important, it offers no evidence on the benefit of safety we seek to estimate. The public's willingness to give or be taxed for other persons' health and safety cannot be measured from any existing data; we can only speculate about it. We can be sure that it is represented by a positive amount greater than present voluntary giving, but we cannot be sure that this amount is large enough to affect X appreciably. In fact, my procedures in this Appendix already implicitly allow for it. In my adjustments to the Thaler-Rosen concept

---

[2] Walter Oi suggested these points to me.

$$X = \frac{\text{extra annual wage for the risky job}}{\text{extra annual risk in the risky job}},$$

I use average worker income *before taxes*. If the ratio of X to the discounted present value of future income is roughly 2, this same ratio or factor is applied as a multiplier to the discounted present value of the worker's future taxes as well as to his disposable personal income. These future taxes represent the interest other taxpayers have in the worker's decisions involving risk, and the application of this multiplier implies that taxpayers in general have the same degree of aversion to a worker's risk of death as he himself has. Such aversion, when included in X, represents a disbenefit of the worker's risk felt by other people. There is no reason to suppose that this implicit allowance is exactly the right one, but I have no better procedure to suggest. The error involved seems likely to be small relative to other uncertainties noted and, if so, is not serious.

The role of various forms of insurance is another possible third-party effect that should be taken into account. Is the compensation for extra risk lowered by the availability of life insurance? Although a failure of premiums charged by life insurance companies to reflect the extra hazards of a job might create such a bias, it is likely to be quite small. The data on life insurance for selected years in Table 10 show that on the average U.S. families carry about two years of income in life insurance of all types for all members (including worker's compensation and the like, though not social security). For a constant income, the average discounted value of future income is at least about eight times annual income. Thus this average coverage is only about one-fourth of the discounted value of the family's future income if income is constant and a smaller fraction where income is growing. Moreover, when family incomes were lower, in 1967 and especially in 1940, the coverage ratio was lower; insurance is a "luxury," rising more than proportionately with increases in income over time. Hence the workers in hazardous jobs, whose average income at $6,600 was below the national average of $8,600, would have a lower than average coverage ratio.

However, the insurance data shown in the table do not include survivors' benefits from social security, which are equivalent, in effect, to life insurance coverage with a fixed premium independent of the riskiness of the worker's job. For a worker with two children the survivors' benefits under 1967 law replaced about half his income until the children finished school; then the benefits stopped until his widow reached age sixty-two, at which time, if not remarried, she received half the payment she would have received on his retirement

TABLE 10

INCOME AND LIFE INSURANCE, U.S. FAMILIES,
1940, 1967, 1970, AND 1973
(dollars)

Year	Life Insurance Coverage per Family	Disposable Personal Income per Family	Ratio
1940	2,700	1,700	1.59
1967	17,100	8,600	1.99
1970	20,700	10,200	2.03
1973	24,400	12,100	2.02

SOURCE: Institute of Life Insurance, *Life Insurance Book* (New York), annual.

if he had survived. Averaged over the worker's entire working life, this set of benefits replaced just over one-fourth of his expected earnings. This replacement fraction is slightly greater than the value of the typical worker's life insurance coverage, so that the two together covered about half the worker's discounted future income. If the worker in a hazardous job had less than average life insurance coverage, the total coverage fraction was less than half. This replacement of income is paid for by taxpayers and insurance policy holders as a group; if the worker survives, this group benefits by avoiding the burden of these payments.

The uncertain understatement of X that may arise from this source is comparatively small. It implies a true value of X higher by something less than $26,000, half the $51,500 given as the discounted value of future earnings. Since presumably workers in the Thaler-Rosen sample had less than the average amount of life insurance and higher life insurance premiums do exist for workers in the most hazardous jobs (so that full compensation for the extra risk would be required to induce workers to accept the jobs), the understatement is $13,000 (for social security) plus at most a few thousand dollars. The value of X given above of $88,000 for a Y/X ratio of 0.2 would thereby be raised into the range of $105,000 to $110,000. At the higher end of this range, the ratio of X to the discounted present value of future earnings, $110,000/$51,500 = 2.14, remains plausible. Since it is doubtful that there is this much bias because of slack in insurance premiums, however, I estimate the adjusted value of X at $105,000 for these workers.

A further technical adjustment is appropriate. The sum of all household incomes is national income; the sum of all final products, net of depreciation of capital, valued at market prices is net national product. Net national product exceeds national income by the amount of indirect business taxes—sales and excise taxes, primarily. The value of the loss of a worker's contribution to output includes these indirect taxes as well as the loss of his income. However, society loses his labor earnings but not his income from other sources. Hence an adjustment should be based on labor income only, not on national income per worker. In 1972–1974 indirect business taxes added an average of 11.5 percent to the value of product; the ratio of national product to national income, on the average, was 1.115. Labor income was about 80 percent of total national income. Hence the indirect business taxes on labor income added 0.8 times 0.115 to the total value of product or about 9 percent; X, as obtained previously, is adjusted by multiplying it by 1.09. Applying this factor to the entirety of X involves an implicit third-party concern for the worker's safety.

A further adjustment is required for direct costs associated with a fatality that are not borne by the family of the victim. Although these items are included in the net national product and so might seem to involve double-counting, it is clearly a gain to society if these costs can be avoided and the resources they represent diverted to something more desirable. On the basis of 1971 data, the National Highway Traffic Safety Administration has estimated that such costs add up to $8,300 per auto accident fatality in 1971 dollars.[3] Although such third-party costs may be different for an on-the-job fatality, I use this figure in the absence of a more exactly representative one.

Bringing the Figures up to Date

Evidence on the value X comes primarily from the Thaler-Rosen study, which used data on earnings in 1967. In the years from 1967 through 1978 average net national product per worker has increased by about 105 percent in current dollars. Most of this increase is due to inflation (see Table 11).

Because of this 105 percent increase in NNP per worker, X is multiplied by 2.05 to obtain its value in 1978 dollars based on current earnings and product levels. A corresponding scale-up of medical and other costs of a fatality borne outside the victim's family raises the $8,300 per fatality to $14,400, based on the rise in the price index of medical care from 1971 to its estimated value for 1978.

[3] U.S. Department of Transportation, National Highway Traffic Safety Administration, *Societal Costs of Motor Vehicle Accidents, Preliminary Report*, April 1972.

TABLE 11
Net National Product per Worker

Year	Labor Force (millions)	Net National Product (NNP) (billions of dollars)	NNP per Worker
1967	80.8	725	8,970
1978[a]	102.0	1,880	18,400

[a] Estimated

SOURCE: 1967 data, *Economic Report of the President.*

Summary of Adjusted Thaler-Rosen Estimates of the Value of X

The data and estimated adjustments I have suggested to reach a representative value of X for the general population are summarized here.

1. Typical value from the Thaler-Rosen Estimates (in 1967 dollars) $200,000
2. Estimated share of this figure for risk of death (the remainder being for injury)   88,000
3. Adjusted value to allow for failure of some life insurance premiums (including worker's compensation) to reflect extra risk of hazardous jobs, and for OASI survivors' benefits: add $17,000   105,000
4. Previous figure multiplied by 1.23 to reflect average worker income in 1967   129,200
5. Adjustment for indirect business taxes: multiply by 1.09   140,800
6. Resulting figure multiplied by 2.05 to reflect increased income from 1967 to 1978 (1978 dollars)   288,600
7. Final adjustment for medical costs and other costs of a fatality borne outside the family: add $14,400 to obtain   303,000

The final estimate of $303,000 is neither the lowest nor the highest possible estimate of X, although it is more likely to err toward the low end of the range.

63

There are many uncertainties in the steps taken to reach this estimate. First, there is uncertainty in the division of the compensation for extra hazards between the risk of death and the risk of injury, and further adjustment could be made for bias because of "free-riding" some of the extra risk on unchanged life insurance premiums. The major purpose of these steps was to give reassurance that the best estimate possible from data on extra wages for extra hazards had a reasonable relationship to the discounted present value of future earnings. The estimate was consistent with this value, but a range of uncertainty remained.

In addition, there is some uncertainty about how to calculate discounted future income for the representative household. In the past, per capita real incomes have risen an average of about 2 percent per year.[4] If the representative household anticipates such growth, as it should, discounted future earnings will be higher. Furthermore, a discount rate of 10 percent is too high for a representative household which has some property income and which is saving and accumulating further wealth. (It is probably about right for workers in hazardous jobs, whose incomes are below average and who probably borrow at relatively high rates of interest.) Suppose, for example, that the household expects a 2 percent annual growth of real income and that its rate of discount for saving-investment decisions is 6 percent. In this case, with a twenty-four year time horizon (at age forty-one), a current income of $10,000 implies a discounted present value of future income of $152,000. By contrast, with a 10 percent discount rate and no expected growth rate the discounted value of $10,000 for twenty-four years is only $89,850.

To obtain an estimate that is assuredly a reasonable, conservative lower bound, the following assumptions could be used: a 10 percent discount rate, no expected growth of future real income, the lowest estimate of X, based on Y/X equal to 0.3, and private life insurance premiums that charge each worker for his added risk. On these assumptions, X is estimated as follows:

1. Minimum estimate of X based on maximum allocation to injuries $69,000
2. Add average discounted value of OASI survivors' benefits, $13,000   82,000
3. Multiply the result times the ratio of NNP per worker in 1978 to average earnings in the Thaler-Rosen sample, $18,400/$6,600   228,600

[4] See Edward F. Denison, *Accounting for United States Economic Growth 1929-1969* (Washington, D.C.: Brookings Institution, 1974), p. 146.

4. Add $14,400 for medical costs and other costs
   borne outside the family   213,000

The result is about $60,000 smaller than the previous, less conservative estimate.

In a similar way, we can start with the upper-limit figure for X using the smallest allocation of the Thaler-Rosen estimate to injuries. The discounted survivors' benefits can be raised by using a lower discount rate and by allowing for expected growth of benefits. These steps give a higher estimate of X, as follows:

1. Maximum estimate of X based on minimum
   allocation to injuries $122,000
2. Add average discounted present value of OASI
   survivors' benefits (6 percent real discount rate,
   2 percent annual growth) plus adjustment for
   failure of some life insurance premiums to reflect extra risk. Total added, $34,000   156,000
3. Multiply the result times the ratio of NNP per
   worker in 1978 to average earnings in the
   Thaler-Rosen sample, $18,400/$6,600   434,900
4. Add $14,400 for medical costs and other costs
   borne outside the family   449,300

In summary, these various assumptions lead to a range of estimates of X (in 1978 dollars) from a low of $243,000, through an intermediate estimate of $303,000, to a high of $449,300, based on the Thaler-Rosen estimates.

Thaler and Rosen reported several estimates with confidence limits around each, based on their standard errors. Broadly speaking, they reported a range of about $60,000 above and below their principal estimate of $200,000, or 30 percent. If we enlarge the range of uncertainty around our final adjusted estimates by this factor, the resulting figures range from a low of $170,000 to a high of $584,000, which is similar to the range for the Blomquist estimates, as noted in the text in connection with Table 5.

Blomquist adjusted his estimates for the risk of injury, and considered the sensitivity of the results to variations in this adjustment. He also showed the sensitivity of his estimates of the value of life to his other assumptions, producing the range of results to which I have applied the adjustments summarized below.

I have adjusted the Blomquist estimates to take into account third-party effects (items 3, 5, and 7 in the above summary of adjustments to the Thaler-Rosen estimates) and to update the estimates to

1978 dollars (item 6 above). In my adjustment for third-party effects, I have used the full $26,000 (1967 dollars) of the insurance premium and social security benefits updated to 1978 dollars to give $53,000.

The full range of results for both Thaler and Rosen and for Blomquist, adjusted for third-party effects and updated to 1978 dollars, is as follows:

	Thaler and Rosen	*Blomquist*	*Combined range*
Low	$170,000	$256,000	$170,000
Intermediate	303,000	409,000	356,000
High	584,000	715,000	715,000

The Thaler-Rosen range includes the effect of their estimated range of uncertainty around their basic estimate of $200,000. The Blomquist range is based on the full range of values he obtained when testing the sensitivity of his results to various assumptions. The combined range (in the final column) takes the low figure based on the Thaler-Rosen estimates, the high figure from the Blomquist study, and the intermediate figure as the average of intermediate estimates.